To Grow in Love

A SPIRITUALITY OF AGEING

Brian Grogan SJ

First published in 2011 by Messenger Publications

Messenger Publications,
37 Lower Leeson Street, Dublin 2
www.messenger.ie

Printed in Ireland

ISBN 978-1-872245-77-5

Designed by Messenger Publications Design Department
Typeset in Myriad Pro

MESSENGER
PUBLICATIONS
JESUITS in IRELAND

Contents

I dedicate this little book to my elders, whose secret scriptures have revealed to me the grace in ageing. I have in mind especially my friends in Cherryfield Lodge, the Irish Jesuit Health Centre, and their devoted carers.

Thanks to the staff of Messenger Publications for their enthusiasm and expertise in producing this book.

Introduction

'All the genuine, deep delight of life
is in showing people the mud-pies you have made;
and life is at its best when we confidingly recommend our mud-pies
to each other's sympathetic consideration' (J M Thorburn).

The image of mud-pies is attractive to me from several points of view. It links in with our origins: we are made from mud (Genesis 2:7) so we get the impression that God likes playing with mud-pies. And the image brings me back to childhood and the delight I found in messing about in mud despite all commands to the contrary. It also catches up how some older people I talk with describe their lives: 'What have I to show for all the years?'

Further, the mud-pie image says something about what I have written in the following pages. St Thomas Aquinas, one of the greatest minds the world has known, remarked at the end of his short life—he died at 49—that all he'd written about God was 'straw' in comparison with the reality. I sometimes felt the same in writing these pages about ageing, because everyone who has reached later life has their own rich experience of what it's like. I can only speak for myself: if I live a decade longer I will view ageing somewhat differently from how I do now. So all I can do is confidingly to commend my mud-pies to your sympathetic consideration, and invite you to construct your own. You have your own chapter, your own unique mud-pie, to add to this book!

I have tried to write primarily from God's point of view, which explains the generous sprinkling of spiritual references. My underlying questions have been: 'What is God trying to make of us in our later years? How can we make some sense of all the diminishment and pain that can accompany them, so that we can come to terms with what seems like loss and decline?' Old age is terrifying to most of us: we need help to navigate it well. Can the often bitter water of these years ever be turned into wine? Occasionally we meet wisdom figures who help us to see the best way forward, people who have come to terms with the reality of their own ageing. They are just themselves; they are not 'difficult'—or at least not for long. Love flows through them to those around, even if they've had a stroke and can hardly talk. If you can find such people, try to be like them. If you can become as they are, you will be a blessing for the world.

I hope that over your lifetime, you have had some experience of God as being good: you need that in order to face the final stage of your journey. If we look back, we can see that our development over the years required us at times to let go of a previous, comfortable stage of life. But the next stage brought something better and was worth the uphill struggle. While we may have resisted, something—or Someone!—was pushing us on till eventually we had to let go of the past. This pushing was for our good—like the pushing involved in giving birth. It helped us to exchange something good for something better. We are pushed out of one comfort zone only to arrive in a new and better one. This process continues in our final years.

With this experience in mind, we can more easily believe that the final push and letting go will bring us something incomparably better than we now have. Only with empty hands can we grasp what is before us. St Paul asserts that 'the sufferings of this present time are not worth comparing with the glory about to be revealed in us' (Romans 8:18). How did he know? He couldn't prove it scientifically, nor can we. But belief in the future goodness of God is based in our experience of God's steady goodness to us over our lifetimes. From God has come to us 'all that is good' (Eucharistic Prayer 4). Old age in one way leads downward, but on the inside, where God is working from, it leads upward into divine life.

Medicine is not always exact. Human error can creep into the most careful treatment. Yet we trust ourselves to surgeons and doctors, hoping that they will make us better and enable us to resume our lives. But an all-wise and good God underpins our spirituality of ageing, so that we can entrust ourselves even more to the ageing process, believing that God will reveal to us new vistas of what human life is about, what 'no eye has seen, nor ear heard, nor the human heart conceived—what God has prepared for those who love him' (1 Corinthians 2:9).

Dance Your Final Years!

'What's Happening?'

For each of us, there is probably a defining moment when we cross the threshold from feeling that we're in 'the prime of life' to the awareness that we're 'not as young as we used to be'. The whiff of mortality assailed *my* nostrils in 2007. I was 69, and had retired from full-time work in administration. I had time of my own; I could do what I wanted with my days. But on Good Friday that year a fire burnt down my Jesuit home. Much of the life I'd known went up in smoke, and a bleak and uncharted future loomed ahead. What was familiar had disappeared—books, writings, notes, bric-a-brac, clothes, photos—and part of me was gone with them. In this time of shock, I knew that I had been rocketed into a new phase of life, with new challenges and surprises. I was being introduced—against my will—to my senior years, the 'Third Age' as it is kindly called. So I am writing from that perspective, and I'm addressing primarily those of you who know ageing from the inside. If you haven't yet entered this strange world, knowledge of its landscape may help you relate more richly to those who have.

Spirituality

The process of ageing happens to everything: to cats and stars and TVs and saucepans, to the universe itself, and to all of us, whether we like it or not. We see ageing all around us; we know what it is. But what about the *spirituality* of ageing? A recent book listed 48 definitions of the term 'spirituality', but let's agree that the spirituality of ageing situates the ageing process *in the context of our relationship with God*. A spirituality is an assertion that there is Another involved in our life. *Christian* spirituality means that *Jesus* interprets our life to us: Buddhists, Jews and humanists interpret ageing differently. Practically it makes an enormous difference to your outlook if you accept the Christian spirituality of ageing: there's all the difference in the world between dancing alone and dancing with a partner! So we will be exploring how we can dance our final years with God, until we enter into the Dance that goes on forever.

'Can I Trust You?'

Can we trust God to stay with us as we age? Does God grow tired of us, or will he truly lead us in the dance of our declining years? Trust is all-important in life, whether you are dancing with a partner, looking for a good friendship, or living out a marriage. The deeper the trust, the more alive your relationship with the other will be, because you can then risk sharing more and more of yourself. Ideally, when you trust someone enough, you can let yourself go completely into that person's arms.

So, if your relationship with God is already a trusting and happy one, you are ready to move along into this new chapter of your life, and even to enjoy it. If you are aware that God loves you through and through, thank God for this transforming realisation: it is not to be taken for granted. As we age we become more dependent, less able to manage for ourselves: we need a helping hand more often. We can entrust our neediness to God if we are at ease with him. But if we feel we can't be sure of God, then we will be afraid to risk this deeper dependence on him. And so I start this book by addressing those of you whose relationship with God has not been so good. My hope is that you will be able to make a leap of trust, or at least to pray: 'I trust you, God, but help my lack of trust'. I also invite you not just to read but to *pray* the content of each article in this book. Ask God what he wants to show you, because God and you are in this process together!

Loved Conditionally?

When I was writing the book *Our Graced Life-stories*, someone said to me: 'I'd love to be in that group'. 'Which group?' I asked. 'I'd love to be one of the people who have a graced life-story!' This was a shock to me: I had taken it for granted that everyone had a graced life story, and only needed to be made more aware of it. In chatting, I found that the person meant that she had little sense of being loved by God. 'And' she said 'there are so many like me. We try to be good, to live out our faith. We attend Mass and so on. We read the letters of Thanksgiving in the *Messenger* and often shed a tear, because we don't really believe that God loves US. After all, why should he?' She continued:

> I feel that God just about tolerates me: he has to because he made me. I go to God to ask for what I need, but I'm afraid. Why? Well, I think that God loves me only if I measure up to his standards, which of course I rarely do. I'm afraid he might get at me through my children—I can stand being hurt myself, but I couldn't stand them being hurt. When I hear someone blithely say to me 'God loves you!' it hurts. I'm sure God pities me, as you'd pity a family outsider, but I doubt he has compassion on me such as I have for my own children. I feel I don't belong. I don't think of God as 'kind'—that for me is love in its truest form. I'm not at home with God—home is a kind word which for me means acceptance, welcome, belonging. Jesus says: 'Make your home in me', but I can't do it. It's a lonely place, to feel left out—the unwanted child.

> I know I bought into what my parents taught me about God, and it wasn't nice. Their acceptance of me was conditional, it was 'iffy'. But if I wasn't good enough for my parents just as I was, how can I be good enough for God? My God was a demanding God.

> But still, that's not the whole story! Over the past while, all sorts of good things have happened to make me doubt my childhood voices. Now I want to let the real God speak for

himself. I've always wanted someone who'd know me—my likes and loves, my fears, my secrets, the deepest parts of me, and I'm trying to risk trusting that God is that Someone who knows me and yet loves me, and that I matter to him. I'm taking baby steps in trust. I pray a lot for that grace. I can't be really alive unless I take that risk.

So I'm in a better place than I was ten years ago. I'm beginning to believe that I'm caught up in a love story with God. In a way I look forward to whatever years I have left, because they'll be happier than the ones gone by. I can see that God is looking out for me in the good things that happen me. Isn't that great? And the flaws of the saints— Augustine and Ignatius and Matt Talbot for example— show me that having flaws isn't a barrier to being close to God. I can be flawed and loved, like an imperfect diamond!

So speaks an honest woman, and since none of us trusts God enough, her story can help us to ask for what we may need. Here we will ask to trust more and more the God who leads us through this mysterious world of ageing.

Conversation with Jesus

Find a comfortable place and a quiet time. Imagine Jesus coming to you: his heart is full. He wants to get across to you just how deeply he and his Father love you. He knocks and comes in: he embraces you. You see in his eyes the message he has for you. You relax, and he says: 'I want to tell you the most important secret you need to know for your later years. It's this: my Father and I will always think of you as our beloved! Our love for you has no conditions. So can you trust us as we walk with you on the path to eternal joy?'

How do you respond?

'God Hasn't Finished with Me Yet!'

Signposts

Last summer, I got lost in the mountains in Austria with two companions. It was towards evening, raining a bit, and the mountainside was getting treacherous; we had used up our food and water, and we were tired. We had no idea where we were, except that we weren't where we wanted to be. We sent up a stark prayer for help. When finally we found a signpost, we were shocked to be so far off course. We still didn't know where we were, but at least we knew the path to take. I still see that reassuring signpost, a lonely sentinel on a wet and barren mountainside.

These chapters on the spirituality of ageing are meant as signposts for what can be a lonely and confusing journey. They intend to offer you a focus. Even if you don't find all the ideas helpful, they may get you into discussion with someone else, and better ideas may emerge. So choose what you find nourishing right now: grace comes tailor-made!

What Do You Want?

So, what do you want now for this time in your life? Reflect on this for a few moments. Remember the first disciples who came to Jesus: he asked them, 'What are you looking for?' If they had replied, 'nothing', St John's Gospel might never have been written. But they said, 'Master, where are you staying?' (John 1:38), and that question, that desire for a signpost, changed their lives. The Lord speaks your name now and asks you, 'What are you looking for? What do you want?' Chat with him about what you want: even if you have to admit you don't know, that's a start. He can take up the running at that point. The main thing is for you and Jesus to be talking to one another!

Make your spirituality personal and vibrant. Spirituality is all about *God and yourself*. It is about the way *you* live out *your* relationship with God. Your spirituality of ageing is unique to you. It is your privilege to work out how you can relate with God in the changing reality of your later years. This book offers some raw materials that I have found helpful for myself, but it's up to you to create *your* masterpiece.

You're Unique!

You may perhaps know much more about ageing than I do. I am 72, and if I live a few years more, I will know more about what I'm talking about here. But by then I may not be able to write, so I'm saying that this is how I see things now.

It is impossible to write about ageing as if 'one size fits all'. We're living longer as a race, and the age group ahead of me is growing faster than any other. Every person within that group is marvellously unique, a first edition. If every baby is different, every older person is much more so, because of how their life histories have shaped them.

Ageing means different things to each of us, and each person will experience the ageing process in particular ways. So if the first chapter in this book was an encouragement to trust God, this one invites you to trust yourself too! Respect your uniqueness as an ageing person, develop a sense of wonder that you are becoming more and more yourself; *you* are mellowing in a way that is different from anyone else, just as I am. Don't let ageing just happen to you: shape it, create it, mould it, put your personal stamp on it! Let you and the Lord work together to form your senior years.

I attended a seminar on ageing many years ago—the intention was that I would be setting up facilities for elderly Jesuits. However, all the other participants were senior citizens: they were attending because they hoped to pick up some tips for themselves. The speaker was an army officer: broad-shouldered, healthy, strong, he had a regular TV slot in which he demonstrated keep-fit exercises. He hadn't checked out his seminar group, so he spoke eloquently about jogging, golfing, swimming, and so forth. When it was all over I asked a nun beside me how she found his presentation. 'Oh Father, isn't he wonderful! He could kill you with one blow!' Doubtless he could, but that fact hardly nourished her spirituality of ageing. So again I emphasize: pick and choose from these pages what helps you to grow old gracefully.

I'm a Work of Art!

In Genesis God is portrayed as addressing his divine council and proposing calmly: 'Let us make humankind in our image' (Genesis 1:26–27). And so God does. St Paul picks up on this: we are, he says, God's work of art, God's handiwork, indeed God's masterpiece (see Ephesians 2:10). But this 'making' doesn't happen to us all at once. We're not like static works of art, rather we're in process. You are meant to be becoming more the image of God as you age. You may say, 'I'm no work of art: look at me—I'm a mess'. You may feel awful, inside and out, but the master craftsman is still busy about you. What you can't do yourself, God is doing in you, now. Your creation is going on today, it is not something over and done with.

The world is a studio, and the Artist is busy about all his projects. You may feel forgotten and therefore miserable, or you may be glad that the chisel and hammer haven't been used on you for a while, though you know that the Artist will be back to perfect his work. You may feel like a piece of pottery that is beginning to crack up. You may on the other hand be catching on to what the Artist is about, and you just hope you're not spoiling things and getting in the way. You may be envious of other works of art in the studio: you can perhaps see in them something they can't see. Let your imagination play on this image of the world as a studio, with God unhurriedly working away, creating you as his work of art today and tomorrow and the next day, till it's complete—the piece done by the master, whose beauty and elegance he acknowledges by signing it with his own name.

Finished!

In the Christian vision of things each of us is completed as a work of art, not on our birth-day but on our death-day. In the emptiness of our dying God adds the final creative touch which completes us. A non-believer attending someone who has just died can say, 'He's finished!' or 'She didn't make it!' A believer will say instead: 'God has completed his work.' Death, then, is not a total dissolution but rather the final stitch which completes a tapestry, or the last dab of paint that makes a great portrait. We become 'a new creation'. (Galatians 6:15)

I stood early one morning in a town in Pakistan outside a dim and smelly shed while I waited for the local bank to open. To my amazement, out of the dark shed were brought beautiful wooden sculptures, shining in the morning sun. This gave me a hint of what is going on in the world—that despite all the chaos of human lives, something beautiful for God is being crafted out of every life. From the chaotic materials of human history the beauty and richness of God's images are drawn, each one revealing something of the genius of the divine artist.

Conversation with Jesus

Sit quietly in your favourite place with another chair opposite you. Imagine Jesus knocking and coming in. He embraces you and then sits down with a loving smile. You are happily surprised at how interested he is in you. But why shouldn't he be? After all you are in a real and mysterious way the image of his Father! Ignatius suggests that, at the beginning of a conversation with the Lord, we might ask: 'How do you see me now?' Jesus will always reply: 'You are my beloved!' (see Romans 1:7). And of course he will call you by your name because you are his (see Isaiah 43:1).

You chat about what you have just read, and the time passes easily ....

Take a Long, Loving Look!

Will They Be Needing Me?

The Dublin author Aidan Mathews tells of an older American who is bored by life and agrees with his wife that he will terminate his existence. She takes this quietly and organizes a large party, no expense spared, so that friends can say good-bye. All goes well, and in the early morning the couple is left alone at the swimming pool, savouring the night's event. After a while silence falls: she breaks it by asking when he intends to 'move on'. More silence; then he says: 'Well, that party was so much fun I think I'll stay around a bit longer'. She cries, but not for him.

Then there's the story of the man who died at 98. At the graveside his widow was chatting with the undertaker. 'What age are you, may I ask?' he inquired. 'Ninety-six', she responded, 'hardly worth my while going home, is that what you're thinking?'

In some western cultures, older people are seen as a problem. The spread of voluntary and assisted euthanasia indicates that some older people and those around them see ageing and its attendant difficulties as undesirable. This can make us senior citizens doubt our own value! For many, the Beatles pose a real question: 'Will you still need me, Will you still feed me, When I'm 64?' And what about 94? Agatha Christie used to say that she enjoyed being married to an archaeologist because the older she got, the more interested he was in her! But most of our friends are not archaeologists, so does their love for us diminish as we age?

Yet in our society, thank God, respect for the ageing is growing: politicians see us as a significant group within the voting population; business people and shop owners recognise our spending power. Elevators and ramps, wheelchair access, kneeling buses, and free travel make our later years more manageable and more enjoyable.

Are You Ageing Nicely?

No matter how others see you, what matters is how you see yourself. Are you content to be your age? Do you feel embarrassed when someone in a bus offers you their seat, or do you smile in gratitude because you feel you're worth it? Can you believe that there's more going on in you than anyone notices? 'Even though our outer nature is wasting away, our inner nature is being renewed day by day' (2 Corinthians 4:16). The fox in Saint-Exupery's tale tells the Little Prince a secret: 'The things that are essential are invisible to the eye!' Those around you, and you yourself too, may see only an ageing person for whom life is running out. But you carry a deep secret: you are an image of God nearing completion. You can grow during this time by learning to see yourself and the world as God does, and by loving others as God loves them.

The experience of being forced to slow down helps this deepening of your spirit. You can no longer do all the things you loved to do, you may feel useless, and time may hang heavily on your hands. But this empty time is a gift from God to be used well. You could indeed spend your remaining days denying your age or grieving that things are no longer the way you liked them. But instead, even if you are ill or infirm, accept God's invitation to explore the unexpected richness of this seemingly empty time. Ageing, whatever its problems, is a blessed time, just like any other phase of your life, and carries its own unique graces and opportunities for development. Days and years of what the psychologist Erik Erikson calls 'a thousand little disgusts' are not God's plan for us.

A Long, Loving Look

The grace hidden in slowing down is that you can become more contemplative: you can give time to seeing and savouring the world as it is. By contemplation I simply mean taking a long, loving look at the real. The real is all around you: it is nature—cats and dogs, insects and flowers, clouds and rain. The real includes your house, your pots and pans, chairs, bed, clothes, and money. The real is human life splashed over the TV screen and the papers—all the amazing things that people get up to. The real is wrinkled skin and failing sight, illness, hospitals, nursing care, infections and drips, smiles, and tears. The real is also the inner world of emotions—worries, fears, joys, griefs, hopes, disappointments, loves, and resentments. The real is the vast world that comes to you through your senses. Take a long loving look at it all.

It may be that you have lived a busy life with little time for yourself. Perhaps you were a mother, busy from dawn to dusk and often during the night too; then you became a grandmother, and when your daughter went out to work you took up your maternal tasks again. Perhaps you spent a lifetime in an office, and when you retired you got to do many of the things you had always wanted to explore. But now God is sending you, in your later years, an invitation to slow down and to ponder. Become a loving observer of God's world around you. You can sit in the kitchen and watch the garden; you can sit in the front room and watch the world go by. If you did the mowing and the digging for umpteen years, take time out now to marvel at the rhythms of life that surround you—grass, flowers, and weeds too, innocently growing, birds at their feeding routines, lights and shades as the day begins and ends.

All the things you have perhaps taken for granted or not had time to enjoy—give them a *long* look now. This is not a waste of time if that look is a *loving look*. Why? Because God too looks long and lovingly at everything: it is all God's handiwork or the handiwork of his people—an autumn leaf, a weed, a TV, a cooker, a newspaper. They all hint at God who is sustaining them in existence right now. So sit with God and gaze lovingly at everything around you. To the contemplative mind, weeds are not simply to be dug out, leaves are not simply to be swept up, children are not simply 'little terrors'. First of all, everything simply *is*! Everything is to be admired. Everything speaks of God, and so by becoming more contemplative you are meeting God, which is what life is meant to be about.

In contemplating life around you, you will be drawn into its mystery—growth, beauty, decay, the rhythms of the seasons, the unpredictable workings of the human mind. You will notice how everything in nature is doing its proper thing. Everything hints at God, 'beauty's self and beauty's giver' as Hopkins says. All creatures are little hints of God. As a great theologian puts it, creation is the monstrance of God.

As you look at all things long and lovingly, thank God for them. Thus you become a grateful person. If the only prayer you ever said was 'Thank you', that would be enough—so says Meister Eckhart. You can imitate Blessed Pierre Favre, the Jesuit who, as he walked the roads of France, used to thank God on behalf of the busy farmers for the crops and cattle in their fields. You can carry a prayer torch for a heedless world. This practice immeasurably enriches your later years, and also enriches the world, in ways you will see only in the world to come.

Take a long, loving look at your own life, too, in its richness and mystery, and thank God for it all. You will come to see that there was more going on in it than you saw at the time, a guiding hand in all that happened to you and in all you did. We will look later at the regrets you have, the dark places where you can't easily see God as yet. It is enough here to repeat the message of the popular story called 'Footprints': during your times of suffering, when you saw only one set of footprints and felt abandoned, it was then that God carried you.

Conversation with Jesus

Once again invite the Lord to spend time with you. Notice him taking a long, loving look at *you*! He does indeed contemplate you, lovingly and humbly, as St Teresa says. He says to you: 'Ageing you may be, but you are still my beloved. I simply love you, from head to toe: the wrinkled skin of your hand, your shaky legs, your thinning grey hair or your bald patch, your forgetful mind, your inability to concentrate in prayer; and most of all I love your heart, crowded as it is with distractions and yet set on me!' Respond as your heart suggests.

Blow the Dust Off Your Trumpet

Stay Alive!

Recently the National Concert Hall in Dublin sent out an invitation to senior citizens who had stopped playing the musical instruments which they had loved earlier in life. They were invited to come along, to blow the dust off their trumpets, and start playing again! Many people did this, shyly at first, but then with more confidence. They had great fun together, and finally got to the point of giving recitals. Most of all, they began to feel that life had regained its colour. This chapter is about ways to stay alive. Like good wine, we can mature with age.

Do you feel the urge to 'blow the dust off your trumpet'? Do you want to have life, and have it abundantly? Do you want to live your days to the full, as Jesus wishes for you (see John 10:10)? Can you allow him to and ask you this personally? Can you imagine yourself as a blossom rather than as an autumn leaf which is slowly curling up and falling apart? Do you experience the temptation to opt out of life by having a predictable timetable and by avoiding risks? Do you say: 'Don't mention an eightieth birthday party to me!' Or as a member of my community once said: 'Sure, a party for me would make everyone happy, but I won't attend.' Do you tend to refuse invitations because they would disturb your established routine? When did you last get your hair done or buy something new to wear? Do you say: 'Sure, that old coat will see me out'? Are you programmed to do the same thing every day and every week?

In an earlier chapter I suggested that our world can be compared to an artist's studio, with the Artist busy about each of his creations, including yourself. Unlike other artists' studios, however, here the works of art are alive, and each is meant to play its part in shaping itself and those around it. Now since we are to 'become like God' who *is* Life, even in our older years we can radiate to the world around us something of the life and the love that God is. We are not meant to fold in on ourselves. By living life as fully as we can, we bring life to those around us, just as they do to us. Certainly it can be a bother sometimes to get in touch with an old friend, arrange to meet, dress up, and go out. But imagine the two of you as God's works of art, who are getting together to see how each is coming along and to encourage one another on the journey. So don't start mouldering yet—leave that for the grave!

But You May Say …

The poem by Jenny Joseph 'When I am an old woman I shall wear purple' is a tribute to the imagination and unpredictability of the older person who is truly alive. It is available in anthologies and on the web. You could write your own version of it, listing the things you'd like to do if you were not constrained by convention. But you may say: 'This stuff is all right for people who still have lots of life in them. But not when you're bed-ridden, not when your energy is sapped by illness and pain, not when you're carrying the weight of family tragedy and loss ….' I fully acknowledge that ageing brings steady diminishment. Where before I climbed up mountains in Austria, now I take a ski-lift to the top and walk down; further down the line I will be happy if I can walk around the block, and finally perhaps I'll get around only if someone pushes me. So we are invited to live life only as we can. That is why I said at the outset that the ideas in these chapters are only signposts. You must choose what helps you in your unique situation at any given time.

But each of us is invited to consider the question: 'What can bring me life right *now*, given my present limitations? What can nourish my body, soul, spirit, mind, at this stage of my life?' I have been told that I must do some exercises daily, or I'll stiffen up. I dislike them; I often omit them; but I know the physiotherapist is right. No pain, no gain. 'If you wake up some morning without pain after 65', a doctor said to me, 'it means you're dead!' So 'staying alive' becomes ever more of a challenge. Again, why bother to watch good TV programmes, read the paper, do the crossword, or go to a film? Because these activities keep my brain active and give me things to talk about. Why bother keeping in touch with friends by phone or email? Because we are made for relationships: we die without them. Why struggle with gadgets such as mobiles and remote controls? Because they keep me in touch with a fast-changing world. Maybe I'm useless with such things, but to close myself off from my available sources of life is to begin to die. The French thinker Pascal said: 'When you cease to learn, you have begun to die'. Recently I heard someone say of an acquaintance who had given up on life: 'She really died years ago, but she never thought to stiffen!'

As we become more dependent, people have to look after us. We can make their task more enjoyable if we are positive, interested in what they're doing, chatty. Family members will tend to visit more if we are cheerful, if we show we love them and care about what's happening for them, if we are intrigued by life itself. Only pure duty will keep a person visiting someone who has given up on life and is self-absorbed and negative. We are alive only when we are reaching out beyond ourselves—life is a relationship with everything around us. People will be attracted to me in so far as I am alive and loving. Even when the lamp of my life burns low, I may manage a smile, a wink.

Oldies and Boldies

Some years ago, the Irish Jesuit Province organized a week-long seminar for its members who had reached 65. They went off to a modest hotel, and for a week were facilitated in exploring what they'd like to do for the rest of their lives. No matter what each came up with, the first response was 'Why not?' The group was dubbed 'the oldies and boldies'—'boldies' because they were willing to shake the dust off their particular trumpets and be fired with a new enthusiasm and zest for life. Their scriptural theme was: 'I have set before you life and death …. Choose life ….' (Deuteronomy 30:19). Their favoured line of poetry was Browning's

'Grow old along with me! The best is yet to be ….' They found the week a liberating experience, they laughed a lot, and they followed through to a greater or lesser extent on what they had imagined for themselves.

Conversation with Jesus

Sitting with Jesus over mugs of coffee at the kitchen table, you might speak with him as did the Jesuit Teilhard de Chardin, who died on Easter Sunday 1955:

> 'Stay with me Lord, because it is almost evening and the day is now nearly over.' (Luke 24:29)
>
> May you keep me always young. What better argument for Christianity could there be than an enduring youthfulness drawn from you?
>
> For old age comes from you,
>
> Old age leads on to you, and
>
> Old age will touch me only in so far as you will.
>
> A smile, inward and outward, means facing with sweetness and gentleness whatever befalls me.
>
> I go forward to meet Him who comes'.

'Nothing added but time' – so runs an ad for a well-known cider. Chat with Jesus about how God's seemingly useless gift of time to you can become grace-filled.

Make Me Grow in Love

'What Do You Want to Be?'

For three years I studied philosophy in the Jesuit House of Studies close to the Grand Canal at Tullabeg, in the heart of Ireland near the Bog of Allen. On Thursdays, our day off, we used to sail an old boat up and down the canal and had great fun. A farming family lived close to the boathouse, and one of the children was asked by a visiting relative what he wanted to be when he grew up—a farmer like his Dad or a truck driver like his big brother? 'No' he said decisively, 'I want to be a philosopher!'

When I turned 72 last year, I mentioned this fact to my spiritual guide. 'So', he said, 'what's your project for the rest of your life?' This was a bit upfront and personal, but it did get me thinking. I began to talk about things I'd like to do: write articles, spend more time with friends, go to the gym more often, pray a bit more, read more poetry, grow things for the fun of it, take life more gently .... When I had run out of steam, he replied 'But what do you want to become, what sort of presence do you want to be in the world?'

I came back six weeks later. We sat in his upstairs room listening to the rain and wind outside. He waited in silence. 'I'd like to be more loving', I said. 'Yes, no matter what happens in the time ahead I'd like to be a loving presence in the world around me. It seems pretty obvious, I suppose .... A bit like Thérèse of Lisieux wanting to be love at the heart of the Church .... Nothing unique about it; it's everyone's call, but I like the feel of it, and nothing else seems quite to fit.'

The Divine Agenda

I said in the previous chapter that it's good to *live* our God-given later years, but I'm very aware that our outer capacity for this diminishes, sometimes slowly, sometimes dramatically. Sooner or later the planned holiday has to be scrapped, and likewise the garden renovation or the gym membership. Life may get narrowed by feebleness, dementia, or whatever. There may come a time when I'll be told that I am terminally ill; then I will have to let go of all my little life projects and turn to more fundamental issues. How can I plan now for what I would want to be then?

The second Eucharistic Prayer has this marvellous line: 'Make us grow in love.' This, the Church tells us, is to be at the heart of our prayer. It's straight from the gospels: 'You shall love the Lord your God with all your heart and with all your soul and with all your mind, and you shall love your neighbour as yourself' (Matthew 22:37–39). This is to be our primary agenda—to become loving persons. But significantly, the Church asks God to make it his agenda for us. The text does not say, '*May* we grow in love' but '*Make* us grow in love'. I like this bit because growing in love is not something we can do on our own—it doesn't just happen in us as ageing does. The daily news shows that many people are given more to hating rather than loving. So our growth in love is primarily God's agenda, but we are meant to collaborate actively and enthusiastically in its achievement.

What's It All about?

Many people seem to go through life without ever asking 'What's it all about? What is meant to be happening to me? Is this all there is?' Imagine being at a meeting where no one knew what the agenda was! It is a huge help to know the divine agenda for ourselves: not growth in wealth or prestige or power, but *growth in love*.

The divine agenda is simple, dreadfully so. You don't have to be a theologian to grasp it. The divine agenda is to bring about a civilisation of love, a world of healthy and loving relationships from which no one is excluded. Each of us is needed to be a carrier of the divine agenda in our situation; each of us is to reveal God's creative love in a unique way.

Imagine a world in which everyone shared this single purpose. Imagine people across the planet getting up in the morning and reminding themselves, 'Now no matter what happens today, I want to grow in love!' It has been calculated that some 85 million meetings take place daily across the world, in the UN, the White House, the Vatican, in parliaments, the courts, local parishes, in families, and between individuals. Imagine that whatever their particular agenda may be, everyone's underlying concern is to do the truly loving thing. How different the TV news would be at the close of such a day!

We can feel that God's agenda of making us grow in love is progressing rather slowly, but blaming God is out of place. I am responsible for *me*: my prayer in these later years is meant to be, 'Whatever happens today, Lord, make me grow in love. Don't let me off the hook.' A friend of mine had a knee replacement recently; the physiotherapy required to get a full bend in the new knee was agonising, but she endured it because the operation would be wasted without the therapy. Life is hard, and old age can be very hard indeed. But God works to bring good out of the pain in our lives, and uses the suffering we cause one another to stretch our hearts to full capacity. Our task is to accept this divine therapy. Jesus learnt through what he suffered, (see Hebrews 2:18) and so can we. It's humbling to feel that I may have been resisting God's work in me over the years, but from today on let me accept the cost of the required enlargement of my heart.

Does It Matter?

One of the blessings of later years is a growing clarity about what really matters and what doesn't. Winning at bridge, insisting on phone calls from your children or grandchildren, always being right and on time, having the last word, being difficult, doing the 'right thing' to maintain your social status—these things can be let go. 'Don't sweat the small stuff' becomes an attractive proposition, and much of the posturing of earlier years can now appear to be small stuff indeed. On the other hand a right level of attention to personal health and appearance, keeping the house or car or garden in good shape, maintaining a social life, being pleasant, being faithful to prayer—such things are good. But deepest down in the jumble of our lives, what *most* matters? 'There is need of only o*ne thing*' says Jesus to Martha who was busy getting his dinner on the table (Luke 10:42). What that 'one thing' is, Jesus doesn't say. But when we look at his life and how he went about 'doing good' (Acts 10.38), we find that this mysterious 'one thing' is that we grow in love.

Many a Wallop

'Batter my heart, three-personed God' says the seventeenth-century poet John Donne. '*Batter* my heart', '*Make* us grow in love'—these are strong words. It's nicer to think that grace is tailored to my needs, and often it is— God often relates with me in just the way I like. But God makes demands on me too, and from being a tailor God can turn sculptor. There's an old Church prayer which says that only with many a wallop does God succeed in shaping us as fit stones for his temple. The shocks, the disappointments, the humiliations, the betrayals and frustrations of my life can be full of meaning. Not that God sets me up for the pain that life provides, but God uses it to stretch my heart and to make me grow in love.

Conversation with Jesus

Sitting in your favourite place with Jesus, you might say: 'Tell me about the painful experiences of your life: the rejections, the betrayals, the physical pain. What helped you through these? Did you sense that your Father was making you grow in love?' What does he say?

Then let him into some painful experiences of your own life. He asks you gently: 'What you have learnt from these hard moments?' Respond as you wish.

At the end, you say: 'Pray for me, Lord, that I may grow in love'. Watch him as he bows his head, closes his eyes, and prays for you. How does that make you feel?

Love of Another Kind

Little Love

In the last chapter we focused on the Church's prayer 'Make us grow in love'. This is what God is steadily trying to do in us. Here we look further at the implications of that prayer. When I was a Jesuit novice back in the 1950s, one of my companions wrote me a poem. It's the only poem that was ever written for me, and I didn't like it! The writer and I were poles apart in style and temperament. My perfectionism, encouraged by the atmosphere of the novitiate, had been getting to him. The immediate occasion of our annoying one another was when he was performing his task of dishing out themes for our May homilies, drawn from the Litany of Our Lady. He handed me a slip reading 'Mystic Rose', and when I protested that no one could talk about that for ten minutes, he offered me 'Tower of David' or 'Tower of Ivory' as alternatives. He went off demolished by my sarcasm. Later that day a poem appeared on my desk. I remember only the following lines:

Sir, nay brother, you are young and cruel:
Just, but with little love;
In all things perfect, save
That in others' faults you cannot see your own.
I love you well,
And yet remember
Christ too was weak,

And did not come to call the just.

I shed salty tears of self-pity over those lines. Here was I, intent on loving God with all my heart and soul, and I was being told in the sweetest way that I had 'little love' for my irritating neighbours! Now, more than a half-century on, am I nearer to becoming the loving person God wishes me to be? How deep and how wide must my love become?

What Sort of Love?

We inch along on the rocky pathway of love. We tend to stop at certain stages and say 'That's as much love as could be asked of anybody …. No one could be expected to put up with more from that person.' Or we say 'I'm getting out of that situation!'—out of the Church, out of a community, out of a marriage or a friendship, out of a parish committee or a job or a commitment. Opting out may indeed be the right thing to do, but am I allowed to close my heart to *the persons* whose inadequacies drove me out?

Look back for a few moments over your life and notice how far you have come on the road of loving. Give yourself credit for all the love you have shown to others. Notice how you have become more compassionate, more generous in reaching out to others, easier about forgiving those who hurt you, and so on. Notice all this laborious growth, and then brace yourself for the realisation that there may yet be more mountains to climb, more miles to go on the path of loving.

The enlargement of our hearts is God's concern. This seems a good idea at first. But if you ask God 'How far does this enlargement have to go?' God will say 'Well, what we have in mind is to make your heart like ours. Is that OK?' We are made for nothing less than God, and God is not someone like us who *has* a loving heart: God simply *is love*—radiant love. There is nothing else mixed in with that love, neither anger nor justice nor resentment. We need images to catch on to this, images which will displace forever our notions of a God who is static and distant, a God who is a mix of great love and stern justice. The image of the sun helps: it simply *is* radiant heat and energy; it gives itself endlessly, helplessly, selflessly. God is boundless, energetic love at the heart of the world and that's where we're meant to be. God is immense love, endlessly active and involved with us. When St Paul says that in the end, God will be all in all (Ephesians 1:10) he means that divine love will finally pervade everything, that the universe will reveal nothing but love in an infinity of delightful ways.

Love of Another Kind

The prayer 'Make us grow in love' can be expressed as 'Make us reveal nothing but love to others'. But this 'love' is a love of quite another kind than we ordinarily understand by the term. In the Christian view, it is not we but God who should decide the measure of our loving. It can't be otherwise, since we are being made in God's own image and likeness throughout our lives. God is love, so God's images must simply be love, not a mix of love and nastiness. It is a great challenge to God to bring this about in us, and a great challenge for us to allow it to happen.

When we ask God to make us grow in love, we can be unclear about exactly what is meant. A friend of mine hired a firm of gardening specialists to give her garden a 'make-over'. She outlined her plans in a general way, but as the week went by she gazed in horror from the kitchen window at the removal of so many shrubs and plants which had become old friends. Where would it all end? But the result was worth the cost: it's now a dream garden. God is that sort of gardener, who strips away whatever is less than love in us. Finally, in our dying, nothing will be left—nothing, that is, except a loving space without boundaries, where God can dwell and from which we can radiate unrestrictedly the divine quality of loving.

Divine Love Is Unique

Over our lifetime, we are meant to become like God. This happens not through growth in creative ability, nor through brilliance of mind or imagination, nor through achievements, but through an expansion of our hearts. Transformation of the heart is the issue. 'This pool of private charity / Shall make its continent an isle, / And roll, a world-embracing sea.' Coventry Patmore's lines state God's agenda: from being focused on personal concerns, our hearts must expand to encompass everyone and everything. Why so? Because that is the special sort of love that

God is. *Agapé* (pronounced 'agapay') is the special Greek term given in the New Testament to that divine love which is directed purely towards others, and which demands no response. This divine love is centred totally and intensely on you and me. It is the divine self-gift to us. This unique love has no conditions or limits: God can't ever become non-loving to anyone, no matter how bad they may be. There is nothing else to which God can resort apart from *agapé*-love. While we can withdraw our love if someone hurts us, and so save ourselves from more pain, God cannot—God is helplessly loving toward us, in the sense that God can't do anything except love us. This is why Jesus compares his Father to the sun: the Father 'makes his sun rise on the evil and on the good, and sends rain on the righteous and on the unrighteous (Matthew 5:45). Sun and rain don't discriminate, nor may we discriminate in our loving. While this is very demanding, it is an endless comfort to know that I am loved thus by God. Nothing I do can make God love me less. God simply is total love for me, and also for everyone else. This *agapé*-love is given to me super-abundantly, and my only task is to share it generously with my neighbours. May I not be the one who cuts off this love from anyone else: this would leave them to a lingering death.

To summarise: this *agapé*-love is uncritical and extravagant—it embraces everyone, good and bad, and embraces me too. It bathes the whole universe. It is pure, transparent, uncontaminated. It is unaffected by human wrong-doing, and it is of its nature forgiving. It never fails; it does not come to an end (1 Corinthians 13:8) It is indeed 'love of another kind'.

Conversation with Jesus

Sitting with Jesus as the Samaritan woman did (see John chapter 4), I say to him: 'Am I becoming a bit more like you in my loving?'

'Yes indeed, you're mellowing nicely!' he says with a twinkle. I listen as he highlights how I have grown in love. His praise melts my heart and I long to mellow even further.

Then he says: 'May I touch on situations where you miss the grace offered and settle for a lesser love?' Only when I whisper 'Yes' does he delicately sketch how I might be more generous, even lavish, in my loving. He explains, too, that this kind of love isn't passive or martyr-like or wimpish. 'It makes demands, it fights injustice, but it's not harsh or conditional. All your negotiations with others need to have around them an aura of endless respect. You can challenge people a lot when they know you love them unconditionally!'

Reveal Your Love to Me

Eyes to See

In the last chapter we said that the quality of God's love is unique, but that God intends to bring to birth in us nothing less than this kind of love. This is what the world needs. Now as we know from being with small children, humans learn by imitation. Every word our parents said, every gesture they made, we watched and tried to imitate. When they smiled, we did so too; when they blessed themselves, we tried to do the same, and so on. We learnt so much then, and this initiation provided for us well through life. But now that we're retired, we are still meant to be learning. 'Continuing education' ideally never ends. Now that we have more time on our hands, can we watch God in the way we used to spend our childhood days watching our parents? Can we try to imitate what we see of his love and so become more truly the images of God? This is real Christian maturing.

Well, if it's true that God loves us totally, do we have any experience of this love? You may say, shaking your head, 'I haven't ever experienced God loving me totally. I've never been blown away by such intense love. If God wants me to grow in love, he needs to show me his own love first. Before we say, "Make us grow in love" Isn't it fair to push God to make us aware how well he loves us? Then we can begin to imitate him!'

This is a fair challenge. Often when I'm with people who are going through life's horrors I wonder why God can't 'zap' them with even a tiny ray of limitless love. Could the curtain not be pulled back an inch or two now, rather than only when the struggle of life is over? These are questions I am storing up for my meeting with God face to face. But in the meantime, clues are scattered all over our lives as to where this love is hidden.

God in Disguise

A first remark is that God, who made us and sustains us, knows what is best for us. There is a world of difference between the initial shy loving glances between a couple and the peak of married love. So it is between God and ourselves. Perhaps God is dealing very gently with us: while he simply loves us through and through and always, we experience this love, not all at once, but bit by bit, since our lives are stretched out in time. We're not angels! God's love is tailored to us; we're not yet ready for its fullness; it would be too much for us. We're still in the courtship phase. We're not empty enough yet for overwhelming experiences of divine love: they would shatter us now. But we will be ready when we meet the Lord face to face.

God Is Truly Good

A second remark is that we *do* know something of this divine love. We find hints and intimations of it as we go along, and we receive it in concrete forms. It comes under all sorts of strange disguises, and mostly we may have missed it, but now we have time to reflect back, to notice and harvest it, and to be amazed. God comes disguised as parent, sibling, friend, teacher, spouse, helper, nurse. God is in those good folk who are dotted over the landscape of our lives and who were or are still 'for us'. God is in those who simply want our good and who perhaps wear themselves out in caring for us, trying to make us a little more comfortable, a little less lonely. Such people unconsciously reveal God's love in a manageable way, appropriate to what we need.

When we were babies, long ago, we took it for granted that our parents should love us totally, meet all our needs, and ensure our happiness and welfare. Such love was so practical, so down to earth, that we can fail to see the mystery of it. But now we can ask: why were we loved so much? Where did that love come from? Can the human heart produce such love of itself, or did it perhaps come from a divine place? The Eucharistic Prayers are clear on the origin of real love. They say: 'from God comes *everything* that is good'. This is a gigantic assertion: whatever good is around me—and in me—comes from God. It's God's way of revealing himself to me as loving, and I can become at least a minor mystic as I begin to see in the love and goodness of others the love and goodness of God.

You Smiled at Me

A third remark can be made. We need to think of divine love from contrasting points of view. There is the soul-shattering experience of love, the kind we call ecstatic, which makes you stand outside yourself. Parents can get carried away in ecstatic love for their newborn child. But there's another side to parental love, and it's shown when the parent gets up every time the baby cries, and does this perhaps for weeks or months or years, in the dark small hours. This is bone-hard love: the parent is still totally 'for' the child, but all feeling may be absent as they endure night after night of broken sleep. The love of Jesus for us on the cross was not an ecstatic but an enduring love, a 'hanging in' sort of love. If you have a debilitating illness right now, you know that 'hanging in' with God doesn't feel like love at all. You're there, you're weak, you feel awful, your prayer is bone dry; but you are 'for God' still, and that's enough. Just as God is set on us, we can be set on God, beyond feeling or sentiment or words. Karl Rahner called this 'wintry spirituality'.

A French mystic summed up God's relationship with her in this short sentence: 'You gazed on me and you smiled'. A smile is so simple: it can say: 'I am totally for you!' Someone once sent me a very plain greeting card saying 'I simply love you!', and that was enough. If God were in the habit of sending cards, that would be their main message. We are meant to rejoice, to give thanks, to dance over the fact that we are so loved by God, however shyly this love is revealed. We are to accept it with open hands and thirsty hearts. Only from this starting place—this living awareness of how well loved we are—can we respond rightly to the challenge to grow into God's love.

Those who have gone before us, 'marked with the sign of faith', can help us. No matter how disastrous life turned out for them, the Hebrews had a deep unshakable conviction that Yahweh loved them. The hard-pressed first Christians are described as rejoicing 'with an indescribable and glorious joy' (1 Peter 1:8) because of the great love shown them in the death and resurrection of Jesus. Life may indeed be hard and cruel. But the kind intentions of God—your creation, your costly redemption, your call to eternal joy—are immovable pillars of the love of God for you. Add all the particular hidden ways in which God cares for you, and allow yourself to be overwhelmed with awareness of how well you are loved. In a thousand disguises God reveals his love to us, and those who are now 'the blessed' work as God's back-up crew!

Conversation with Jesus

Gazing at Jesus sitting across from you, pray as St Catherine of Siena did. She asked him to reveal himself as he promised when he said: 'Those who love me will be loved by my Father, and I will love them and *reveal myself* to them' (John 14:21).

In reply he may say: 'I will be delighted to do that, but let's notice ways in which I already reveal myself and my love in your life.

He invites you to think of your body, and of the beauty of nature and the cosmos in their wonderful mystery. Hear him say: 'All of these reveal me to you in their different ways'. Then he adds: 'Recall all the persons who have enriched your life. I gave them to you because I love you!' Next he says: 'In becoming human I revealed myself fully to you, as much as any person can reveal themselves to another. The Gospels are a revelation of who I am. And there's nothing I like more than this sort of conversation or prayer we're having right now, when you reveal yourself to me and I reveal to you what's on my heart.'

He speaks of the Eucharist as the daily revelation of his love for you. 'The bread is broken, the blood is shed, *for you*! I love *you* and give myself *for you*' (see Galatians 2:20).

He gazes on you and he smiles .... Smile back in return! Take in what you can, and wait patiently for the close of your life when you will meet him 'face to face' (1 Corinthians 13:12).

The Prayer of a Tired Pilgrim

All or Nothing?

At dinner one evening, our Jesuit community got to talking about prayer and its difficulties. Our eldest, who was 82, stayed silent for a while, and finally said: 'Well, I can't talk about my prayer. Either I'm praying all the time or I'm not praying at all!' Many older people may find comfort in that remark: I certainly do, and more so as the years slip past. Jesuits do an annual eight-day retreat: I used to divide each day diligently into four or five hour-long prayer sessions; I'd work my way methodically through selected materials, and report daily to my guide on progress achieved. But now that plan doesn't work too well. I can still allot the prayer periods: the time goes by but where have I been? What progress can I report? On the other hand, when I relax and go for a walk, I find I'm in the same attitude toward God as I was in the formal prayer times. So in our later years, is it all prayer or no prayer? What's going on?

What's Prayer About?

Life is a relationship: God is the big partner and we're the small ones. God has a project for us: to make us grow in love. When we're starting out on this relationship, we spend time getting to know him, his values, his intentions for us. We do this mainly through watching his Son in the

Gospel scenes, and so we become somewhat like him. Bit by bit, and not without struggles, we develop the same mindset that Christ Jesus had (see Philippians 2:4). Time spent in prayer of this sort gives us the occasional sense of achievement, as we find ourselves becoming a bit less selfish, a bit more open to unpleasant people, a bit more concerned about the poor, a bit easier in forgiving those who wrong us, a bit more patient in bearing suffering, and so forth.

At this stage, prayer times have a clarity about them: we want to have the mind and heart of Christ Jesus: we see this goal out ahead and we inch toward it. But gradually there develops a harmony, a closeness between what we are and what God wants us to be. So then things get a bit blurred. It's one thing to see the sea from a mountain-top, and quite another experience to be swimming in it. There's less to say about it because it's too close. If someone shouted to us 'What's it like out there?' what would we say? 'Well, there are waves all round: they're blue when the sun shines, grey in cloud, choppy in the wind .... That's about it ....'

Too Close to See

Is our journey of prayer a bit like that? We pray because we have a yearning for God. Meeting with God in prayer changes us, so we become a bit more like God. The change shows in a mellowing of our hearts and minds. Real prayer makes us more loving, and so God is getting his work done during prayer. But while busy in our prayer, God is also busy in our lives, and is labouring in every detail to make us grow in love, outside our prayer. We are being brought too close to God to be able to see him. Things become indistinct, we don't quite know where we are, just as when we sail out of sight of land. This loss of the familiar can be frightening, which is why amateur sailors try to keep the coast in view. And this brings us back to the older Jesuit who was saying: 'I don't know where I am: either I'm praying all the time or I'm not praying at all!' When you have become a loving person, you have become like God, and so the distinctions between you and God get somewhat blurred. You have arrived into God's domain. Your prayer and life merge into a single yearning for God.

Going with the Flow

You'll probably say at this point: 'He can't be talking about me!' But I am. And I hope I have encouraged you to believe that your prayer, such as it is, is not a waste of God's time. The question is not: 'Am I a person of great prayer?' You're probably not, if you think that praying means long periods of undivided concentration on God. Instead, the issue is: are you trying to be more loving? To that question you can answer at least a tentative and humble 'Yes!' If in doubt, ask a friend. The command has been given: love the Lord with all your heart, and your neighbour as yourself. Over a lifetime, through ups and downs, successes and failures, you have tried to obey this command. By now you should have a larger heart. You're more accommodating of people, more tolerant, less critical; you've given in to God's arrangements for your life. You're less stressed because you're not obsessed with your own importance. People can let you down or do what you'd prefer they wouldn't do, but they're no longer running up against you, because that earlier self-important you is disappearing. You're cruising now rather than pushing against the tide; you spend less time being resentful, hurt, frustrated; you give more time to gratitude. Also you have integrated to some degree the sadnesses and regrets of the years, and left their resolution with God. While you're still a work in progress, you are on your way.

How to Pray Now

Prayer is a loving conversation with God by whom we know we are loved: so says St Teresa. Ignatius echoes this and speaks of prayer as a conversation between two friends, in which we talk about what occurs to us, and notice how God responds. You can chat with God about anything, because you believe he is interested in every bit of your life. And since God is also interested in what happens to everyone else, you can talk to him about them, and this will help you to relate lovingly to them. You find yourself growing in love for yourself, for others, and indeed for the whole world, because your Friend loves them. You watch the TV news, not as a detached spectator but as one who cares about everyone, both perpetrators and victims. You can breathe a prayer for each of them as the news moves along. A fuzzy sort of prayer grows in you, in which you wish everyone well. You thank God for the good in them and you ask him to undo the bad in them.

A senior citizen recently said to me that her prayer seems often to go like this: 'God bless everyone, Lord; those I love, and those I don't: no exceptions. And God bless Yourself: you've a hard job with all of us. Look after us all. Amen.' Further enquiry yielded the following: 'Well, I'd be wanting God all the time, the way I'd be wanting my husband back, and him dead eight years now. I've less and less idea what God looks like, but I'm wanting him more and more.' Perhaps she speaks for many of us: we try to pray because we yearn for God in an indistinct but total way. God has no boundaries we can grasp. 'O God, you are my God, I seek you, my soul thirsts for you; my flesh faints for you, as in a dry and weary land where there is no water' (Psalms 63:1). This sort of prayer has been called 'the prayer of stupidity' because you can't say anything coherent about it. It seems to have no content. But it is enough that you want God: if God appeared you'd be delighted, but since he hasn't come yet, you wait for him, even if impatiently and distractedly.

Conversation with Jesus

Watch Jesus through the window as he arrives. Sense how he looks forward to these meetings. His smile assures you that he enjoys your company. Chat with him …

'Jesus, I love our chats, and also our silences. If they are what we mean by prayer, I'm happy. It's you I want! And I try to accept each day as you set it before me. I've changed a lot: I try now to go with the flow and let you lead me on. As you bring me toward the evening of my life, make me praise you and grow more and more in gratitude.'

How does he respond?

'God, Do You Really Care?'

From a Distance?

Does God care? We often wonder about this, especially when things go wrong. The song says: 'God is watching us … from a distance'. We can tend to think that this is how it is—God in his heaven, watching us, but from a distance. But if this book means anything, then the opposite is the case. God is very close indeed, keeping us and everything else in being; God is active in our world, shaping and reshaping it endlessly in response to our choices. When our choices are flawed, God weaves them into a new design in his tapestry. This is what we mean by divine Providence. In our later years, as things seem to fall apart and the demon of doubt nibbles away at our old certainties about God, it is important to keep in mind that God cares endlessly about us and works for us indefatigably with all the energy of his divine love.

An Open Project

It helps if we appreciate that God's design for the world is not rigid but flexible; it is more like a football manager's game-plan than an architect's blueprint. It's an open project. A friend of mine said to a kitchen designer: 'Make this kitchen over: work out the colours, the tiles, the location of the bits and pieces. So long as it's bright and airy and things are within easy reach I don't mind. I trust you not to make a mess of it.' Likewise

God gives us freedom to create a harmonious world in which everyone is respected and cherished. Although we persist in making a tragic mess of it by ignoring the guidelines given, God does not abandon the divine project. Easter celebrates how God reverses the catastrophe we create; God brings to birth a new and totally unpredictable beauty and harmony, but not without great cost. God cares infinitely about us and never abandons our world. God's dream works out every so slowly through history, but God will get us home in the end.

'Am I Boring You?'

I can ask God: 'What are you thinking right now about me in my present condition? Are you bored with me? Are you interested in my pain, my sorrows? Are you like a dutiful nurse who knows I haven't long to live, and who's just trying to make me comfortable and ease my passing? Are you giving me palliative care rather than a cure? Are you angry with me because, after more than eighty years, my faith is weak? Do you think of me as a failure when you hear me admitting to friends that I find it harder and harder to believe in the next life? You know, Lord, the silence of my dead spouse and of many friends is deafening to me, and I often think: suppose there's nothing after death? Suppose you're not going to be there to welcome me?'

What God Might Say

Might God respond: 'I'm right here with you. I know what is going on in you, your doubts and fears, your loneliness, your regrets. Your life till now was crowded with all sorts of challenges—education, job, marriage, family, sickness …. Now that you are slowing down, there's more time for us to meet, and I'm glad of that. It's like being in a popular restaurant in the late evening, when the other diners have departed and there's just the two of us. This is our chance for the heart to heart conversations I've wanted. Can you believe that I am the God of Life, and that I simply want you and everyone else to become fully alive? Sickness, suffering, pain, sin and death were never part of my dream for the world. I deal carefully with these tragic realities to bring life out of them but I admit it takes a long time to resolve them.'

Your Final Stage of Growth

'This time is your final stage of growth, although it feels much more like a time of decay and decline. This is a time of great grace for you—my love is active all around you and in what happens to you. It's a time for the final cleansing of your heart of whatever is opposed to love. Then you will be completely filled with my New Life. You are becoming what you were always destined to be: my image and likeness.

I'm holding you by the hand, drawing you forward into something new. This body that served you well but is now worn out and painful is to be let go. You are being made ready for a new life. All of this preparation is hidden: outsiders can't see it. But I am orchestrating it. In all the letting go, I am bringing you closer to myself, and freeing you from all that stands in the way. So don't lose faith in me, no matter how hard life is now. This life is a back-stage preparation for the real play which comes after you die!

Unless the Grain Dies

You may protest: 'But, Lord, what of all the useless effort in my life? My family, for instance: they didn't turn out the way I'd wanted. I tried to give them a good example, but it seems to have come to nothing …' Would God respond gently: 'Yes, I know because I watched you, and supported you in your efforts. You wonder whether I care. I know I'm mysterious. Much of what you did may not bear fruit in your lifetime. So it was for Jesus: he died without seeing the fruit of his efforts. Only at the end of history will you see the marvellous outcome of your good deeds, your sincere prayer, your generous sacrifices. Don't grow tired of doing good, for in due time you will reap a rich harvest (see Galatians 6:9). Together you and I are walking toward a future beyond describing: take my hand for the remainder of the journey and we will come home together!'

Two Good Women

But you're not quite convinced yet. You might say: 'Lord, I feel I have achieved so little with my life. I'm like the widow in the Gospel who had only two coins to put into the Temple treasury, or like that woman in the Russian story who was laughed at by her neighbours because she gave everything away. She left behind her only a rubber plant and an old goat and …'

And can you let the Lord reply? 'Yes, but you're forgetting the last parts of those two stories. I praised that woman in the Gospel because she'd put in all she had, and you can do that, even now: just entrust your life to me and I'll keep it safe. And the Russian woman was also praised: the author said of her that she was the sort of woman without whom no village could live, and no town or city, and no country. I want you, like her, to love the world with a great love, and to be kind to all the people you meet. Can I ask you not to take yourself too seriously? Laugh over your mud-pies! You may think you haven't much to show for a lifetime, you may feel that your life is falling apart, but what you and I have accomplished lovingly together will be revealed in eternal life.'

Conversation with Jesus

When you are comfortable in your favourite place with the Lord, you can continue the dialogue you have just read. Perhaps too you can make your own this prayer adapted from Teilhard de Chardin. Here he prays for the gift of trust in the caring Providence of God.

> Grant, Lord, when my hour comes, that I may recognise you in the diminishments of my later years. When age begins to mark my body, and still more my mind, when the illness that is to diminish me or carry me off strikes from without or within; when I awaken to the fact that I am ill or growing old; and above all at that last moment when I lose all control and am passive within the hands of the great unknown forces that have formed me; in all those dark moments, O God, grant that I may understand that it is you who are freeing me in order to bear me away to yourself. Teach me, Lord, to treat my death as an act of communion with you.

Redeem Your Regrets!

No Regrets

Sigrid Undset's epic tale *Kristin Lavransdatter* is set in fourteenth-century Norway. Kristin is a headstrong and beautiful child, her father's favourite, but she betrays his love in her early teens by having an affair with the attractive but unstable Erlend, whom she marries. They have seven sons and while she loves them all, rearing them stretches her heart to breaking point. Erlend squanders their property, becomes distanced from Kristin, and dies from a wound received in a brawl. When her daughter-in-law takes over the running of the family home, Kristin realises that she is not wanted any more. She joins a nunnery as the Black Death sweeps through Europe. Through an act of charity to a poor person she contracts the plague herself and dies an agonizing death.

As she lies dying, Kristin reflects on her life, a mix of wantonness, pride, and hard-heartedness, as well as maternal love, generosity, and repentance. Focusing on her wedding ring,

> … her tears burst forth in a swift stream, for it seemed to her that never before had she understood to the full what it betokened. The life that ring had wed her to, that she had complained against, had murmured at, had raged at and defied—none the less she had loved it so, joyed in it so, both in good days and evil, that not one day had there been when 'twould not have seemed hard to give it

back to God, nor one grief that she would have forgone without regret.

What to Do with Regrets

Not one grief that she would have forgone without regret!

In a previous chapter, I invited you to share some of the difficult experiences of your life with the Lord, and to let him take you through them. You may well have been painfully reminded of situations which you regret—perhaps a failed marriage, a distancing from one of your family, a lost friendship, a betrayal of trust, a bad decision. Perhaps you feel now that life hasn't been fair to you, that things just didn't work out, or that a hasty decision did irreparable damage.

What can you do with such regrets? You can choose to let them fester: but then you grow depressed, negative, bitter, so that you end up being turned away from God and from those around you. The alternative is to take a long, loving look at them, and to hand them over to God now, rather than postponing this to your deathbed. God's love for us is big enough and God's hands are close enough to enfold even our darkest situations. 'Can a woman forget her nursing child, or show no compassion for the child of her womb? Even these may forget, yet I will not forget you. See, I have inscribed you on the palms of my hands …' (Isaiah 49:14–16). Surely these are among the most comforting verses in Scripture.

Blessed Are Those Who Mourn

'Blessed are those who mourn'. How could Jesus say that? He immediately adds 'for they will be comforted' (Matthew 5:4). We mourn so many things. First there are those things about which we can do nothing because they are outside our control. Loss of health is an example, or the death of a loved one, or an ecological disaster. But we can do one thing! We can entrust them to God and ask him to bring good out of them. This stretches our faith: can we believe that the God who sustains all things in being can and will restore what has been spoiled or lost? We who mourn are blessed because we shall be comforted either now or later by God's bringing good out of every disgrace. Nothing good will be lost. The dead will rise, our friends will be restored to us, every tear will be wiped away, a new heaven and earth will shine out, all things will be made new (see Revelation 21:1–7). We are promised that the darkness cannot overcome the light (see John 1:5). Promises are the language of divine love.

What I Did and Failed to Do

But what about things that were in my control and that I have spoiled? I have misused some of my gifts, I have hurt others, I haven't been available to people in their need. When I look back now at relationships that went wrong, I can rarely say I was totally innocent. Will I live my remaining years in a cloud of frustrated regret? 'If only I had reached out …. If only I'd been a bit more sensitive …' Is it too late to hope that my discordant notes can somehow be fitted into God's symphony of the universe? No, it is never too late!

The memory of my failings can inspire a change of heart in me. From the damage done something good may flower. Alice was fifteen when she and her eight-year-old brother Hans were pushed into a train bound for Auschwitz. She saw he was missing a shoe. 'Why are you so stupid?' she shouted at him. 'Can't you ever keep track of your things?' Then they were separated and she never saw him again. Broken-hearted, she vowed never, ever to say or do anything that could not happily stand as the last thing by which she'd want someone to remember her.

But we can't undo the original damage we did. The little boy Hans died in the gas-chamber without ever hearing his sister say 'sorry'. Ultimately only God can heal all wounds, and as creatures we must entrust into his healing hands the harm we have done. The psalmist has the lovely line: 'You have kept count of my tossings, put my tears in your bottle. Are they not in your record?' (Psalm 56:8). This offers the image of a God who cares, who treasures our tears, and who, heaven alone knows how, will resolve the world's pain.

Light out of Darkness

We're touching here on the mystery of how God copes with human failure and evil. At the heart of the darkness is a gleam of light that can give us hope. This gleam of light is the awareness that God works endlessly to bring good out of evil. Here God is at his most mysterious, but mysterious in a good way. The primary example of his bringing good out of evil is when Bad Friday became Good Friday. The horror of the day remains: it should never have happened; nothing can justify it. But God brought good out of it by revealing the limitlessness of divine love in the face of human malice. We are to learn from this that the characteristic labour of God is to bring good out of evil.

Occasionally we see these gleams of light in others' lives and in our own; not everywhere, but often enough to give hope that God is at work in the darkness. I know families bereaved by the tragic death of one of the children: they are softer, gentler, more caring with one another now. They have a new compassion for similarly affected families. The pain of a broken marriage has opened up some of my friends to a wider love. The horror of clerical sexual abuse is leading to a humbled Church. We can thus believe that the damage we do, our crucifixion of one another, is redeemed not by us, but by God's creative activity. He is the master craftsman who delights in restoring his damaged masterpieces. Awareness of this can bring peace to our troubled hearts. The dying Kristin of our opening story is brought to see this: 'there was not one grief that she would have forgone without regret', because God brought great good out of each of them. Something fresh and new was born which would not have been there otherwise.

A final regret which is to be redeemed is the feeling that the love and care you gave to someone has not borne fruit—a prodigal child has gone astray, alienated despite all the love you lavished on them. St Paul consoles the Galatians who felt this way: 'Let us not grow weary in doing what is right, for we will reap at harvest time, if we do not give up' (Galatians 6:9). Love endures eternally and will reap its reward, so entrust these regrets into God's hands too.

Conversation with Jesus

Ask Jesus to help you to understand the extraordinary prayer of a Jew who died in Auschwitz during the Holocaust:

> Lord, when you enter your glory, do not remember only people of good will.
>
> Remember also those of ill will.
>
> Do not remember their cruelty and their violence.
>
> Instead be mindful of the fruits we bore because of what they did to us.
>
> Remember the patience of some and the courage of others.
>
> Recall the camaraderie, humility, fidelity, and greatness of soul which they awoke in us.
>
> And grant, O Lord, that the fruits we bore may one day be their redemption.

In the quiet, Jesus says gently: 'No suffering need ever be wasted. I surround it with divine love and work to transform it. Thus your own sufferings and those you cause to others become the occasions of great good. But you'll see this fully only when human history is brought to a close.'

Give Me a Forgiving Heart

Unfinished Business

Michael was a respected teaching brother, who was popular with most people and had held responsible positions in his religious congregation. However, he and Alex, another member of his congregation, had an intense dislike of one another. They had run a school together, but had disagreed bitterly for many years, not over trivial things but about educational policy, treatment of staff, and so forth. They tended to avoid one another at congregational gatherings, celebrations, and funerals. And so the years went by.

Then came news that Michael was terminally ill. Alex was a little shocked to notice in himself a hint of satisfaction when he heard of Michael's plight. Being retired he had plenty of time—more than he wanted—to reflect on the years of his relationship with Michael. He found himself agitated and disturbed: whenever he tried to pray, a picture came before his mind of Michael fading away into darkness, like a TV being switched off. The angers and hurts of the years played around in his heart together with a sense of self-righteousness—events had in fact proved that Alex had been in the right all along.

One day at Mass, Alex heard the celebrant alluding to Ignatius' question at the time of his conversion: 'What ought I do for Christ?' With searing clarity he saw what *he* ought to do. He drove to the convalescent centre, but went first to its Oratory. There he prayed the purest prayer he had uttered for years: 'God, have pity on us both!' When he went in to the sick man's room he saw a look of fear on Michael's shrunken face. He took his bony hand and said: 'Michael, I had to come: may God have pity on us both!' They cried a little, and between the tears they looked at one another and each knew he was forgiven and accepted. They talked of silly things—of golf and horses and how the school was doing and of funny 'senior moments'. Alex would have hugged and kissed Michael but couldn't. At the end they both said 'Thanks' and cried a little more. Michael died a few days later.

Forgive Them!

Perhaps there is someone you can't forgive? Perhaps, like Alex, you now have more time than you want to brood over the injury someone caused you? Be kind to yourself: to have the desire to forgive may be as far as you can go, and that is enough for now. The history of humankind is one of violence; others can hurt us terribly; and it may be far beyond us to forgive them. How can Jews forgive those responsible for the Holocaust? All we can do is pray for the strength to want to forgive. Total forgiveness requires a deep compassion for the other person, and that may take years to achieve, as in Alex's case. Note too that when we want to forgive but haven't the words for it, even a single phrase can suffice, as between Alex and Michael. If words can't be used, a glance, a handshake can suffice to absolve a world of bad feeling.

Forgiving Love

If we were left to ourselves, forgiveness would be even rarer than it is in our world. But we are not left to ourselves! God wants our forgiving to match the limitlessness of divine forgiveness. God is revealed as pure love who never holds anything against us. The parable of the Prodigal Son (Luke 15) presents Jesus' favourite image of his Father's forgiving heart: no scolding, no conditional pardon, no demanding a full and abject confession, no punishment. Those who heard the parable must have thought that the father was mad. They would say, 'No self-respecting Jewish father should act like that'. Yet such is God, and God's forgiving attitude is to be the mark of a genuine Christian. Until by grace we reach this point of reckless forgiveness we are not ready to fully enjoy God's company.

It is a great comfort to realise that forgiving love is at the heart of our tragic world. It gives us hope for ourselves, and sets up an ideal for us to imitate. We talked before about the kind of love that God *is*—*agapé*-love, which is such a special dimension of loving. It is pure, other-directed love, endlessly self-giving even if there is no response. This love is undeterred by human malice. God simply loves us and wishes us well. Forgiveness is a quality built into God's sort of loving. The dark shadows of resentment which Alex found buried in himself when he thought of Michael are absent in God. God is a God of reconciliation, and the kingdom of God is a reconciled community. The dream of the three divine Persons for the final great wedding feast is that when they beam delightedly at all their guests, they will see each of them beaming at all the others. Each of the divine Persons works endlessly for this, and slowly, ever so slowly, they win us round.

Jesus' Love

The previous paragraphs could be dismissed as wishful thinking were it not for the quality of forgiveness which Jesus shows. A sceptic who knows nothing about the New Testament might say: 'All this stuff about God's forgiving love is the product of an over-heated pious mind. You're saying what you'd like to be true—wouldn't we all wish to be forgiven? But prove it!' You might ask your sceptic friend what he would accept as proof. Suppose he said, 'Well, if your God were to enter human life with all its vulnerability, if he suffered at the hands of others as we all do, if he forgave them, and if he came back to them after his death and told them a message of forgiveness and pardon—then I might be convinced'.

This is of course what Christian faith is all about. We don't know God the Father at all well, but we know the Son: the Son reveals to us perfectly what his Father is like and 'has made him known' (John 1:18). We talked earlier about becoming images of God: the Son is the perfect image of his Father. He knows exactly what his Father is like, how he feels about us. As we said above, he sketches in the parable of the Prodigal Son the staggering nature of his Father's forgiveness: no recrimination, no condemnation, no punishment: instead, total forgiveness and lavish restoration of his son's lost dignity. His joy is simply to have his son back. But Jesus goes beyond words to reveal divine love: in the torture of the Passion he reveals himself as Forgiving Love in action. This revelation of the forgiving love of God is what makes the Passion worthwhile. Father and Son were then able to say: 'Now people will know that we never hold anything against them, and that's good'.

He's Looking at Me!

We can say: 'This is great! Isn't it very consoling that God is like that. There's hope for me yet!' And there is! But the snag is that God wants us to become like himself. Ours must become a limitless compassion for those who have not yet reached the fulness of love which God intends for them. God needs us to play our part in creating his dreamed-of community of reconciliation. The great wedding feast would be a sad affair indeed if the guests haven't forgiven one another. So if God's love for us is a forgiving love, our love for others must be the same. God asks us to forgive those who have wronged us, and keeps nudging our stubborn hearts, as he was nudging Alex in the story above, until we give in. If we do, there is great joy in heaven: so long as we don't, God has more work to do in us before we are revealed as his masterpieces.

Conversation with Jesus

When you and Jesus have chatted about lighter things, perhaps take your crucifix and gaze on it for a while. You might say: 'Lord, don't let me be the one who blocks your work and the flow of divine love. Help me let go of grudges. Help me to shape a kinder world here and now by forgiving those who have hurt me. Push me as you pushed Alex. Please give me a forgiving heart now, because so long as I refuse to forgive, I'm part of your problem!'

Sense the silence for a few moments. What does Jesus then say to you?

The Meaning Comes Later

'If I hear anyone talk to me again about letting go, I'll let go all right—I'll hit them!' So said a friend who was enduring more than her fair share of difficulties all at once. So we too may often feel. Relinquishing mobility, status, work, health, and so on, doesn't come without anguish. In a spirituality of ageing we have to try to make some sense of the painful reality of letting go.

The first illusion to be let go is the idea that God is simply 'nice'. God, who is love itself, can of course be nice, but can also be a demanding God, and even, we may feel, unfair. We are forced to let go of childhood images of God as a Santa Claus, who gives us all we want and makes us and our loved ones safe and happy always.

God, we have said already, has an agenda for us. That agenda is our growth in love, but not love as measured by human standards. The stakes are higher: our love has to match that of God, nothing less than that. We are to become like him: that is the demand. God makes use of everything to achieve this agenda. He intervenes directly in our lives, and also uses the interventions of others, both helpful and unhelpful, to achieve his purposes. God does not cause suffering and evil, but draws good out of them. God works only for our good, and does so by transforming evil from inside. Sometimes we can see this happening; most often we can't. What is disastrous to us while it's happening can later turn out to have been worthwhile. I was ruled out of contention for a job once because of arthritis: I was upset at the time, but later realised that the job wouldn't have been right for me.

'You do not know now what I am doing, but later you will understand' (John 13:7). So says Jesus to Peter, who can't allow his Master to take the role of a slave by washing his feet. This seems to be a basic rhythm of our lives: often, like Peter, we can't see the point of things at the time, but if we reflect later we may see how they fit in. The more we catch on to the fact that the meaning comes later, the easier it is to 'let go and let God'.

'Wow!' Moments

Occasionally I get to chat with a friend who is a contemplative nun. She intersperses the conversation every now and then with the quiet comment 'Wow!' Sometimes her 'Wow!' is saying 'Well done, Lord!' when a problem has worked out surprisingly well. At other times it is an acknowledgement of the sheer mystery of what's happening: it's then a shorthand for 'Over to you, Lord!' Either way, her interjection hints at a perceived connection between human affairs and the world of God. It's her way of expressing her belief that God is at work in everything, both good and not so good. This belief makes it easier for her to go with the flow of life. For her, life is not just a bundle of facts, pleasant, painful, or boring: rather, it is an all-embracing symphony, of which she consistently hears the underlying melody. It is helpful to find people like that: they have a steadying message for us when life seems to be falling apart and all seems lost.

Letting Be

A member of my community died after three months of cancer. He was seven years younger than me, and kept doing a full day's work even when he knew he was dying. I asked him one day what he thought of St Ignatius' comment that sickness is no less a gift than health. He looked out the window and said 'Huh? Try it yourself and see!' That closed the conversation, and he got on with his heavy task of letting go of his unfinished life. I have slowly come to see that my occasional sicknesses and surgeries have brought good to me. They have helped me to get a better perspective on things. By putting a halt to my gallop, they have made me a bit more sensitive to what others go through. Thomas à Kempis in the *Imitation of Christ* states that few are improved by illness, but I am always amazed at the patience which blossoms in many people as they endure sickness and old age. There's endless letting go, but something else is given—resignation, acceptance, inner peace, courage, and radiance. 'Even though our outer nature is wasting away, our inner nature is being renewed day by day'. (2 Corinthians 4:16)

As we age we are invited to accept the rhythm of letting go in order to receive something better. This rhythm has in fact characterized our lives from the beginning, though its focus sharpens as we age. We didn't want to be born, yet life outside turned out to be even better than life within the womb. Childhood was a happy time, but we had to let it go to enjoy our teenage years, and their freedom had to yield to the responsibilities of adult life. Marriage and parenting meant the letting go of personal freedoms, but if the relationship went well, the rewards were great. And now that we're growing old, the process continues. The best is yet to be, and the best is God, who is infinite happiness and works to make us ready to share that with him.

Jesus' Letting Go

When we contemplate the Passion of Jesus, we touch on the great 'Wow!' moment of human history. Here God is most magnificently at work, bringing good out of extreme human evil. What went on in Jesus is called his self-emptying or *kenosis* (Philippians 2:6–11). He chose to empty himself, first by becoming human, then by accepting his dreadful death. In the garden we are given a privileged glimpse of how he struggled to let go patiently and trustingly. He knows all about letting go! The resurrection was his reward, and the saving of us all.

The pattern of Jesus' life is meant to be repeated in us. The letting go of our later years culminates in that total letting go which we call death. We don't choose this painful process: we endure it. We don't *choose* enfeeblement or being marginalised or being considered a nuisance. But while Jesus' *kenosis* came primarily from inside, our being emptied out starts from outside. Bad things happen to us and we can't avoid them. Thus Jesus warns his friend Peter: 'When you grow old, you will stretch out your hands, and someone else will fasten a belt around you, and take you where you do not wish to go' (John 21:18). The mode of his death will be imposed on him as it is on each of us. Our *kenosis* goes on inexorably, with or without our consent. Yet we have a role to play in it. We must decide either to accept our diminishments gracefully, or to resent and reject them. We can turn our diminishments and our dying into a positive, creative, and loving decision: 'Lord, I accept whatever is to come!'

This is the road of grace, the road that Jesus took. The core of a healthy spirituality of ageing lies here: firstly, to let go of what is being taken from us; then to let the resulting emptiness be; and lastly, to let something new grow in us. To illustrate: friends of mine found that their first child was incurably blind. They have had to let go so much of their hopes for him. What amazes me is how they have come to terms with his reality, and how new depths of love have grown in them. He will never see them, but he reads their faces with his fingers, and that is enough.

Conversation with Jesus

Seated across from my friend, I look back with him at what I have had to let go over the years. I say: 'Help me, Lord, to see what good has come from all this letting go. Make me more gracious about all that is now being taken away from me. Don't let me be a source of pain to those who stay around me. Instead of being negative, let me be a sign of hope to others that you hollow us out only to fill us with yourself. Let me witness that you remove what is not divine in us, and in due time will fill our empty cups to overflowing'.

He takes my hands, looks into my eyes, and responds … I listen with rapt attention.

God is Very Close

'God Went Away'

> I've lost any sense of God being close. Years ago I used to feel that God was near me: I can remember when I had Sophie, my first child, holding her for hours on end and feeling myself enveloped in God's love, just as I was enveloping her in my love. But that's long gone. There isn't much love in my life now … husband dead, children married and living a long way away, occasional visits from a diminishing circle of friends …. So where's God?

Many older people experience this sense of losing God: what you may notice is that God is gone behind a cloud or to another place; there's a sign on his door marked 'Gone Away'. You may find life difficult, and you may have little sense that God hears your prayer—so much of it goes unanswered. It's not that you want to ask too much, but you feel that a little sunbeam or a hug might not be amiss, or a little let-up on the difficulties that plague you. But strangely you don't give up on God and close your account with him. This is crucial in the spirituality of ageing.

Dark Night

It can help to know that the 'dark night' spoken of by mystics is not restricted to monasteries. Something similar comes over your home too. First comes twilight, then night, then dark night. Familiar landmarks fade, such as the quiet trust that God is close and caring. You may find yourself in the dark night without any discernible occasion such as severe illness, tragedy, or depression. The ageing process brings you into its own world of sadness and difficulty: enfeeblement, loss of faculties, the departure of friends, isolation, dependence on others, sense of personal irrelevance, and so forth.

Well-meaning friends can try to talk us out of this experience of the absence of God. But the dark night is not an illness like TB to be cured: it's more like chemotherapy, which is necessary for our long-term health. It is a purifying time, a time for pure faith and trust in God. God is indeed still with us, but in the dark, so that we cannot see him.

Heart Transplants

What is God doing? In an earlier chapter we said that God's work in us is to 'make us grow in love'. This work of God is painful to us. It involves the stretching of our small hearts to breaking point, a hollowing out of our souls so that they can be filled with God. To be filled with God means to become alive with God's own love, that pure and other-directed goodwill which we called *agapé*-love. The critical questions about loving are: 'Can I let God love me unconditionally? Next, am I growing in that unconditional love for myself and others? Am I making space for others in my heart? Do I wish them well, no matter how shabbily they live out their lives? And then, am I beginning to pray for those whom I tend to despise—useless politicians, business people who live at the expense of others, people who don't treat me respectfully?' Radical surgery is required in us even to *want* to love our neighbour as ourselves (see Matthew 22:37). We spoke before of the need we have for *larger hearts*, but perhaps instead we need *heart transplants*! Would that do for a description of a Christian? 'Real Christians are people who have undergone heart transplants, they know how limitlessly they are loved by God, and now they try to love everyone else as fully as they love themselves.' St Paul says that when anyone has been grasped by Christ, there is 'a new creation' (Galatians 6:15). It is the heart that must become this new creation.

However we imagine the process, making each of us grow in love is the work of God and this invasive procedure disorientates us. We are jolted out of our comfort zones: it will no longer do to say 'I'm basically a nice person: I love my friends: I try not to make life difficult for anyone—I keep the commandments and so on, I read the *Messenger* and I'd never miss Mass, all of which—to be fair to myself—is more than many people do!' If we dared to say all this to God, God might respond:

> OK, this is a good place to start. Now we'll get you into training, so that you'll be able to love everyone around you, the good, the bad, and the ugly! You see, I don't just love the good people and tolerate the bad specimens: I happen to love them all: I wish them well, I do all I can to make them grow in love. I want you to include them within your love and concern, these unpleasant brothers and sisters of yours. Why should Abraham intercede for the unworthy sinners in the doomed city of Sodom (Genesis 18:23–33)? Because I put him up to it! You see, I'm determined to save *everyone* and bring them home, and I need your help. Anyone who is failing in love is a concern of mine, and my concerns must become yours too! This will bring you and me into full harmony. Let's get you up to speed on this sort of loving—OK? But it will be demanding for you. It isn't cosmetic surgery, it's inner work—heart stuff!

And so the conversation might proceed—or rather, since you'd be tongue-tied by God's agenda, it might be a divine monologue. All you can do is nod your assent as the surgeon prepares to go to work. Then you realise that there's no anaesthetist!

As you lie there, your mind is saying: 'This isn't the God I used to know! This is a tough God! My little world was so neat: those I'm nice to and those I'm not—the good versus the undesirables. What will I be able to gossip about when I can't take sweet enjoyment in the failings of others? I'll have nothing to say! And if heaven is packed with those I call undesirable, how comfortable will I feel?'

The Intimacy of God

Good images can help us to trust that God hasn't gone away but is working in us. The image of the dark night helps: although we can no longer see God, he is there, but hidden. The psalmist talks of God's intimate work in forming us in the womb (Psalm 139): this work still goes on: we are slowly coming to full term in the womb of God. Moses reminds the Hebrews of this care of God: 'You saw how the Lord your God carried you, just as one carries a child, all the way that you travelled until you reached this place .... The Lord your God .... goes before you on the way, to seek out a place for you to camp, in fire by night, and in the cloud by day, to show you the route you should take.' (Deuteronomy 1:31–33) God is an unobtrusive support, a fellow-traveller, not a distant observer.

St Augustine picks up the issue of God's hiddenness within us. He says, 'God is nearer to me than I am to myself: God is inside, while I am outside'. Because God is working on me from the inside out, I can't see what is going on. Teilhard de Chardin uses the image of the divine hands. With one hand God holds me carefully, with the other he shapes the universe. I am held securely and shaped, even if I don't know what is going on. Hopkins says that God is 'nearer to me than breathing /and closer than hands or feet'. How intimate and close up that is! Merton says that God dwells in our deepest core and cannot be dislodged by our sinning: from that intimate place God shapes our lives. So our creation is ongoing: our hidden God is using everything, both good and bad, in our lives, to make us grow in love, each in our own unique way. His masterpieces will be fully revealed only at the end, but even now we can radiate something of the love which God is.

Conversation with Jesus

When you and your friend are comfortably together, continue the conversation begun in this chapter. You might say: 'Don't let me spoil what you are trying to do in me. Let me interpret the good and happy side of my life as your work, since 'from you comes

everything that is good'. And let me believe that in the painful sides of my life you are also quietly labouring to hollow me out and fill me with your love'.

How does he respond?

Who Cares for the Carers?

Ruth

My aunt Nellie was a passionate dancer; she fell in love with a band leader from Belfast in the 1920s, and when they married she moved up north. He had been a Presbyterian, but joined the Catholic Church soon after the marriage. He worked in the Harland and Wolff shipyard, but once it became known that he had converted, he was never offered promotion and his salary remained at a low level. The couple had two daughters and sacrificed all to rear them well. Kathleen joined the Dominicans and taught in Belfast until her retirement, soon after which she died of cancer. Ruth went into business, but devoted all her spare time to looking after her parents as they became infirm. Eventually, the demands of caring made her give up her job and also the prospect of marriage. So the years went by and her parents eventually died. She found new work, but then began to grow frail herself. There is no one to look after her: now in her eighties and almost blind, she lives in sheltered accommodation, supported by a few staunch friends.

Ruth was a carer, long before the word came into vogue. Her story is in no way unique: many did what she did, and please God people will always step forward to care for relatives and friends, even at great cost to themselves. Society is only now coming to realise what a debt it owes to carers. Perhaps you were a carer yourself? Perhaps now you are fortunate enough to have someone caring for you?

While our focus here is on carers of the ageing, carers are needed too at other phases of life. Our parents were our primary carers: they tended us with love from infancy until we became independent. If you married, your partner and yourself cared for one another. Doctors and nursing staff care for us through illnesses and surgery. Perhaps you, like Ruth, cared for an ageing parent, or looked after your grandchildren to ease the burden on their parents. Caring is of the essence of human and Christian living: ours is a caring God who invites us to share his task.

The importance of a spirituality of carers is not yet well recognised. What interior vision can be offered to carers, to sustain and motivate them? How can they be helped to find God in the selfless work they do?

Escorts of Grace

Earlier we spoke of the extraordinary quality of God's own love for us, a love that is selfless and totally directed towards us. God simply wishes us well and never acts but for our good, no matter how we respond. Carers can imitate that divine example of loving to a greater or lesser degree. God wants to reveal his love through them. They are to be his hands and feet, his voice and smile. People who are cared for are blessed if they feel this generous love. 'Christ has no body now but yours, no hands, no feet on earth but yours.' This reflection attributed to St Teresa of Avila could be a hymn for carers. The three divine Persons are totally supportive of the carer. Most obviously the Son offers them the supreme example of caring: he cares for everyone, even to death, for 'No one has greater love than this, to lay down one's life for one's friends' (John 15:13). The Father and the Spirit are active in carers' lives too: God's love has been poured into their hearts by the Holy Spirit that has been given to them (see Romans 5:5). Carers, then, don't go to work alone: the three Divine Persons travel along with them. It is a caring God who inspires and energizes all carers, whether they know it or not.

Close to God

Carers, then, are very close to the Lord, and the spirituality of caring is based on this truth. Like Jesus they can reveal by their love what the

Father is like. This may seem an impossible ideal: but essentially it means always to wish well to those to whom they minister, to respect them even when they're frustrating or unkind. It means to see them as the 'beloveds of God' (Romans 1:7) and not as 'cases'. Such attitudes make great demands on their inner resources: carers are invited to see these demands as God's way of making them grow in love. Caring carries a stamp of divine appreciation: 'I have seen all that you have done in secret and I will reward you. Because I was sick and you took care of me, inherit the kingdom prepared for you from the foundation of the world' (see Matthew 6:6 and 25:34–36).

Jesus himself had his carers: his parents acted this role, as later did the women who travelled with him (see Luke 8:3). At Bethany his carer was the woman who anointed his feet (see John 12:3) and after his death those men who took him down from the cross and placed him in a tomb. Finally in this procession of carers are the women who came to anoint him on Easter morning (see Mark 16:1). To say the least, Jesus must have a soft spot for carers! And what must have gone on in these simple folk when they discovered that they had been caring for the Son of God!

What Do You See?

The film *Patch Adams* is based on a true story. In it Robin Williams plays a mature medical student whose style of relating to psychiatric patients draws down the wrath of his teachers. His class had been told: 'We train the humanity out of you here!' But instead of treating them as 'cases' he takes them seriously as persons. He respects their often weird ideas and behaviour and makes them smile. They find in him someone who is on their side, understands them, and actually likes their company. The student on whose life the film is based went on to found a truly caring facility for awkward patients written off by the medical world. Beyond externals he saw the mystery of each one.

Carers then can nourish their spirituality by seeing every patient as an unique reflection of the face of God, a divine mystery, an unfinished work of divine art, someone who will in good time shine like the morning star (see 2 Peter 1:19 and Philippians 2:15). The carer's secret task and privilege is to help God develop each person as a masterpiece. A carer is meant to be an escort of grace to each patient. In doing this the carers themselves become God's masterpieces. Those who tend others often say: 'I get more from them than I give'. This is the Christian way of things: grace flows between people who respect one another: it is not one-way traffic : we are both givers and receivers all at once, because grace is rich and relational.

'Help Him Yourself!'

I was shocked into realising how uncompromising is the Christian command to care, when I spent some time in Somalia thirty years ago. I visited what passed for a hospital. The facilities were minimal: no running water, hardly any medicine. A man was writhing in agony from third degree burns: another patient was fanning him, but the nurses ignored him. With some gestures and a few words of Somali I asked them to help him. 'No, he is not of our tribe!' they replied. 'But you must help him' I begged. One of them turned on me: 'You're a Christian: help him yourself!' I became aware as never before of the scope of the Christian challenge to love. The carer's life can be hard, as our opening story illustrates. Voluntary carers especially may lose out on so much: social life, career, marriage, health itself. The heart of a true carer will be emptied out of personal ambition but instead 'will be filled with all the fullness of God' (Ephesians 3:19) which is not a bad exchange!

Conversation with Jesus

As you chat with him, you see him as the Great Carer, the one who cares for us all, through our lives and deaths and into eternal joy. Hear him say gently: 'I will always care for you in a way that is special to you'. Savour how that makes you feel.

Then you ask him: 'How can I be a bit more like you in my own caring?'

He might reply: 'Bring the person you are caring for into your relationship with me. Imagine they're here at table with us. This won't make a disagreeable person pleasant—though it just might—but it will widen your heart. Without a divine depth of love there will be an edge to what you do, no matter how professionally good you are. You can't change other people, but I'll help you to change your attitude to them. I used to remind myself that my Father loved all the people to whom I ministered, so I came to see each of them as images of God, multiplied but not monotonous, distorted but not to be despised'.

When I start to do this I notice the difference it makes: I thank him then for this gift.

When I Breathe, I Am Praying

I Can't Pray!

As we age and when we are sick, a feeling of uselessness can grow on us. This may bring on a sense of depression. We used to be able to do so many things; now we find that we can be looking out the window for hours, doing nothing, getting nowhere. We can then feel guilty. 'I have all this time on my hands, and yet I can't pray. When I was younger I was very busy and gave hardly any time to prayer. But I used to promise God I'd give him plenty of time when I was older. Now I have endless empty hours on my hands, but where's the prayer?'

Each of the previous chapters has concluded with a conversation with Jesus. I suggest that you pray that way when you can, following St Teresa's idea of prayer as a loving conversation with God who totally loves us. St Ignatius takes the same line: 'Imagine Christ Our Lord present before you upon the cross, and begin to speak with him ....' But we can't pray like that all the time, so how can we enrich the idle hours in which we seem to be able to do nothing?

The suggestion in this chapter is that we can link prayer to our breathing. Nothing could be simpler than this. Breathing can be seen as a holy action, and when you know this, it eases the struggle of trying to pray when you can't focus and when you can't stir your heart to loving attention.

Wrapped in Silence

Sit in your favourite place, your sacred space, where you have perhaps a little statue or an icon and a candle. Or if you're confined to bed, think of your bed as a holy place. Recall the story of Jacob when he was on the run from his brother: he lay down, exhausted, put his head on a stone and fell asleep. He dreamt of a ladder there, on which angels are ascending and descending. God came and spoke comforting words of promise to him. When Jacob woke up, he said: 'Surely the Lord is in this place—and I did not know it' (Genesis 28: 10–17). So God comes to your place of rest also. God has your address and likes to visit, even at odd hours!

Allow yourself now to become still. Listen to any sounds around you. Let this listening grow deeper. You can hear sounds only because you are quiet. If you were talking, you wouldn't notice them. Become more and more a still point in a turning and noisy world. The quieter you become, the more you hear. The Lord comes very quietly. As Tagore wrote: 'Have you not heard his silent steps? He comes, comes, ever comes.' Our Lady was wrapped in silence and listened to what was going on in her heart. Invite her to be with you: she will help you to become quieter.

Now notice your breathing: gently inhale and exhale. Imagine the scene in Genesis: God breathes into your lifeless body and you begin to stir with life (Genesis 2:7). God's breath becomes the breath of your life! Your breath is indeed your own, but it is also God's. Some day your breath will cease, so it is precious: it keeps you going. For the first time in your life, perhaps, make a silent prayer of gratitude to God for your breath.

YAHWEH

Now I want to develop an idea from the Franciscan writer Richard Rohr. Think of the word YAHWEH. It is the most sacred word of a pious Hebrew; it is the name that God utters when asked by Moses who he is (see Exodus 3:15). It is a word endlessly rich in meaning: it says that God, who is above all names, is solidly present to us, close to us, on our side. YAHWEH is the God who is full of tenderness and compassion, and this God is in our corner, fighting for us. Jesus would have learnt the word YAHWEH from his parents and then breathed it with awe and reverence.

YAHWEH, then, is a beautiful word, full of hope and comfort. But more: it mysteriously matches the rhythm of your breathing. Notice the sound of the word Yah-Weh. If you gasp for a moment and listen to your breathing, you will notice that as you breathe out, you are making the sound 'yah', and as you breathe in, you are making the sound 'weh'.

As you breathe, you breathe out and in the name of God, YAHWEH, the One whom you try to love above all else. So when you are conscious of your breathing, you can make it a prayer. But even when you're not attending to your breathing, this little mantra is being sung in your body: it is like background music, and you can come back to it easily.

Instead of imagining that you are far from God when you can't focus on him, now let your breathing do some holy work for you. Let your breath carry your prayer: it tells of the longing, the yearning of your being, which is for God. You just want God, and that is enough. Don't worry because you can't focus on God: you can't focus on air either! God is beyond images and words. He is simply the endless desire of your heart. 'O God, you are my God, for you I long: my body pines for you, like a dry, weary land without water' (Psalms 63:1, Grail version).

A Chinese tradition holds that we come into this world with the gift of a certain number of breaths. When they are used up we expire. Long life would then mean breathing gently and slowly, rather than hurriedly. Breaths are precious! What makes them double precious is that we can grow in our relationship with God by matching the sacred word YAH-WEH with the rhythm of our breathing.

On Standby

So you are potentially praying so long as you are breathing! God gives you your breath moment by moment. Offer it back as a sign of your commitment to him. Include it in your morning offering with the prayers, works and sufferings of the day. You desire to be given over totally to God. Often you are unconscious of your breath and of the sound it makes, which is the sound YAH-WEH. But every so often what is unconscious becomes conscious, and you articulate and re-affirm the prayer hidden in your breath. You will find it consoling to feel that you are in prayerful mode every moment of your day, even when you doze during a time of prayer.

We Pray with our Bodies

You may have to overcome the idea that we pray only with our souls and that the body is irrelevant. But our souls express themselves through our bodies. Monks pray with their bodies when they stand and sit and sing the psalms for hours each day. They also believe that to work with the intention of serving God is to pray. Ignatius of Loyola would enthusiastically agree. Augustine remarks that those who sing, pray twice. We bow our bodies in adoration. We join our hands and bless our bodies with them. We receive the host at communion and eat it. We go on pilgrimage, which is a bodily prayer. Truly the body prays, because it is as a human person, body and soul, and not as an angel, that you meet your God. You won't hear God saying: 'Now, when you pray, please leave your body behind you. I'm interested only in your soul!'

My mother had a stroke in her mid-seventies and died four years later. I was there that morning, with a friend, when her breathing began to grow more drawn out. She would breathe out, and then there would be an impossibly long pause before she breathed in again. Finally she breathed out, and we waited, transfixed, for her to breathe in again. Not daring to breathe ourselves, we waited five, ten, twenty, thirty seconds, a minute … But no breath came. She was gone. For those who love God, their final breath, conscious or not, matches the prayer of Jesus when he says: 'Father, into your hands I commend my spirit' (Luke 23:46). His Father had been the desire of his whole being throughout his life, even when he was busy or sleeping. The Father can be so also for us, even as concentration declines in our later years. There is a website named 'Pray as You Go': the suggestion in this chapter is 'Pray as You Breathe!' Try it.

Prayer Has Already Begun in Me

Bad Nights

In this chapter we will fill out the background to the previous one. We said that by the very act of breathing we are already praying in a real sense, and that we can make our breathing more deeply prayerful by using the word YAH-WEH as we breathe out and in. As the years pass, it can be a comfort to know that we need not worry so much about the quality of our prayer. We can simply pray in harmony with our bodies.

I seldom become conscious of my breathing during the day, but during sleepless nights I do. Then, at least occasionally, I silently link my breathing with the holy sound of YAH-WEH, and something is salvaged from a 'bad' night. Several of my brethren have suffered from emphysema: they know how much effort breathing takes. Surely this discomfort is already a prayer of sorts? Surely it is precious to the God who gave them breath and will receive it lovingly back when they die? If our tears are stored in God's flask, our breaths are too!

My Heart a Temple

It is encouraging to know that contemplatives say prayer has already begun in us long before we become aware of it. The place where God dwells in me is also the place of prayer. I am a temple of the Holy Spirit (1 Corinthians 3:16). The three divine Persons dwell there, and they relate lovingly with each other and with me, which is what prayer is all about. While I occasionally give myself to prayer, the Holy Spirit never ceases to pray within me 'and intercedes [for me] with sighs too deep for words' (Romans 8:26). That means that the Spirit is addressing the Father and the Son, and does so in the cathedral of my heart and on my behalf. That prayer is my heart's treasure, even if I know little about it. Right from the beginning of my life, prayer—this conversation of the Three—has already begun. It is present before I do anything: it lies deeper than any of my techniques or my efforts to 'pray well'. Think of a newborn child, whose parents talk about it lovingly as soon as it arrives. Well, even before my baptism this prayer of the heart has been going on, although the sacrament highlights the intimacy of God in our hearts. Prayer is there—just as breathing is there independently of my thinking about it. Prayer, the monks say, just goes on and on.

'To live in the state of grace' means that so long as I want to be a friend of God, I live in a state of prayer at a deep level. I will grow in my relationship with God by learning about prayer, which is the discovery that Someone is in love with me! That Someone has been in my life always, but I only slowly become aware of them, and of their goodness. Prayer is waking up to this mysterious reality that I am *the beloved of God* (Romans 1:7). The three divine Persons have already taken up residence in the depth of my heart. Growth in prayer occurs when I join in and become part of their conversation, their 'prayer'.

'They Love Me!'

If you had good parents, can you remember when you woke up to the fact that your parents loved you—that they'd been loving you long before you were born? That they had always wanted you, just as you? That they'd put themselves out in endless ways over the years for you, but had done so happily? That giving them space in your heart and in your life is right and good? Or think of a friend: can you remember the day they told you that they loved you, and had been loving you for a long time? Prayer is a time of waking up to the fact that you are infinitely loved, and it leads naturally to a loving response. Why should God love me? Just because God is like that, and I'm grateful.

For a fortunate child, the love of parents is simply there, all the time, through good times and bad, whether the child is aware of it or not. And the love in the lover's heart is simply there, waiting patiently for the beloved to become aware of it. So too in our hearts the prayer of the three divine Persons is simply there, endlessly. For us it is a blessing when we get into tune with the divine music of love in our hearts.

Like this antecedent love of parents and of God, our breath is there, from our first moment to our last. So this prayer of the heart and the breath of our bodies have much in common. They go on even when we know nothing of them. Breathing and praying have been going on in us since the nurse or doctor got our first breath going. In our full reality of body and spirit we have always been a sanctuary for prayer. Speaking silently or aloud the name YAH-WEH to the rhythm of our breathing brings this prayer of the heart to consciousness. That is a cheering thought.

Conversation with Jesus

Focus on the sanctuary of your heart; it is a temple, graced by the presence of your Lord. Settle down and become still, listening to the sounds and become aware of yourself as a point of stillness. Attend to your breathing, and silently speak the sound 'YAH' with your outgoing breath, and the sound 'WEH' as you breathe in. You will gently become aware that God is with you already, even before Jesus shows up.

Now let your imagination play for a moment! Listen out for the sound of Jesus' coming: the footfall on the gravel outside, the knock on the door, the smile and chuckle of his greeting. But when you look at him, you gasp in astonishment: he has become old. His hair and beard are grey, the freshness has gone from his cheeks, which are sunken; his skin is wrinkled. He comes in more slowly than before; he's got a stoop. But despite the wrinkles, the eyes are the same; his gaze is even deeper and more understanding, more accepting, more loving. The smile is still there, and it is more expansive than ever before.

Tears come to your eyes. How could it be that he has grown old? You have a flashback to a film where the beautiful heroine goes through an ordeal and emerges as an old woman. Your mind is in turmoil, but his calmness gradually settles you, as if he were saying: 'Don't be afraid. All is well!'

And then it hits you! He has become like you: he is the same age as you are! Love makes like, and now you know in a new way how much he loves you. He became human like you, after all, and is like you in every respect (see Hebrews 2:17)and he has been carrying you along your pilgrim path over all the years. He loves you as you are, and he shows you this by becoming as you are now.

He takes your hand and caresses it with his own. The skin is mottled and hangs loose, but the grip is still firm, and the clasp is warm and comforting. You and he gaze into each other's eyes and search each other's face. There is no need for words. 'He comes, comes, ever comes', and it's true. Here he is, melting into your life situation, just as you are. And you do as invited by another poet: 'I greet him the days I meet him, and bless when I understand' (Hopkins).

Love Bids Me Welcome

In this book we have explored together, from a Christian point of view, various aspects of ageing. Now it is time to reflect briefly on dying and how to face it, 'so that we may not grieve as others do who have no hope' (1 Thessalonians 4:13). Death can be terrifying to many people because they imagine it as an endless falling into darkness, but we are offered the 'sure and certain hope' that Jesus, our life-companion, will be waiting there to welcome us. I will use a good deal of Scripture in this chapter, so that you can feel secure that its ideas are based not on naive optimism, but on the unfailing promises of God.

Welcome!

As I come towards my final days in this world, Love bids me welcome. Love drew me out of nothingness when the universe began. I was chosen even then to be holy, and to live through love in God's presence (see Ephesians 1:4). St Elizabeth of the Trinity says: 'There is a being whose name is Love, who longs for your company'. This mysterious Lover, who has smiled on me all the days of my life, gazes now on me in my pain, confusion and weakness, and still smiles on me. I will be safe in this love, this welcoming smile. God does not change. I am always 'God's Beloved' (Romans 1:7).

Saying 'Yes' to God

God smiles on me. I try to smile in return, though I may be in great distress. 'Blessed are you who weep now, for you will laugh' (Luke 6:21). Death involves tears, but here we are given the promise that joyous laughter will follow soon after it. My dying should be a self-giving: a total handing over of myself into loving hands. They *are* loving hands, for on their palms my very own name is inscribed (see Isaiah 49:16). And recall Chardin who says that with one hand God shapes the universe: with the other hand God holds me carefully.

Let me then in good time say to God, 'Into your hands I commend my spirit' (Luke 23:46). Jesus said this just before dying, but he lived thus always. The whole dynamism of his life was focussed on his Father. He was made over to the Father from the beginning. Perhaps this prayer of Jesus has been your prayer since you began to notice that you were not as young as you used to be: if so, that is good. But perhaps you will be helped by beginning to say it now. In the third Eucharistic Prayer we ask that Jesus may make us 'an everlasting gift' to the Father. Let us now generously hand ourselves over to God in a free personal act of self-giving.

A Spirituality of Dying

Thus a Christian spirituality of ageing merges into a spirituality of dying. A smile, inward but also outward if possible, can capture my loving response to God. As an 'everlasting gift' let me attach a smile to the gift! This is the time for my final self-donation. 'I give myself to you!' Towards the close of *King Lear* the devoted son Edgar tells his father, Gloucester: 'Ripeness is all'. Ripeness indeed is all. Ripeness of heart is an acceptance of what is to come. To die well is a task, a hard task for some, but Jesus gives us his example to follow.

The Jesuit Superior General, Pedro Arrupe, was disabled by a severe stroke ten years before his death in 1991. He composed the following prayerful farewell address to his brother-Jesuits in 1983, by which time he was unable to speak. The words were read aloud for him. They have helped many senior Jesuits and others to hand themselves over to God in their later years, and they may help you!

More than ever, I find myself in the hands of God. This is what I have wanted all my life, from my youth. But now there is a difference: the initiative is entirely with God. It is indeed a profound spiritual experience to know and feel myself so totally in God's hands.

God Comes, Comes ...

For me as a Christian, dying is an inter-personal event, the most sacred event of my life. My dying is not simply a 'systems failure'. I do not know the how or the where of my death. But I know who my future is! I do not die alone only later to find myself ushered into the presence of God. Rather, God comes for me, God makes a journey of love to my bedside. God hurries, like the father who runs toward his prodigal son and catches him up in a loving hug. God comes for me as a bridegroom comes for his bride. God guides me 'through the darkest valley' (Psalm 23:4) into his own wonderful light. His promise is firm: 'I will come again and will take you to myself, so that where I am, there you may be also' (John 14:3). Could Jesus do more to ease my fear of dying than this? My beloved will say to me: 'Arise, my love, my fair one, and come away, for now the winter is past, the rain is over and gone' (Song of Songs 2:10). God then comes for me, takes me by the hand and leads me home.

C. S. Lewis said of his wife, Joy, as she died: 'She smiled, but not at me'. Many people smile as they die, they smile at God who is there, but whom only they can see. They smile because they recognise God and what God has prepared for them, which passes all imagining (see 1 Corinthians 2:9). Around my bed will be some family members and friends, perhaps a nurse too. But behind them will be the three divine Persons, who are radiating toward me love beyond all telling. They are proud of me, wasted and worn though I am. They know my heart, they are delighted that I have grown in love. Their work in me is nearing completion, the surprising work of art which I am is now close to perfection. I am almost ready to enjoy the company of all those blessed ones gone before me, who already experience the multiple overwhelmings of God's gracious love.

Sure and Certain Hope

Christians have an unique perspective on death. I spoke of the 'sure and certain hope' that Jesus offers, the promise that indeed, all will be well.

But the shadow side of death looms large. People rightly ask: 'Will I wake up after dying?' Our Christian faith is founded on the belief, based on Jesus' own resurrection, that death is not the end. With the coming of Christ an unquenchable light shines in the darkness of death (see John 1:5). We say at Mass: 'Dying you *destroyed* our death, rising you restored our life'. The Gospels are all about the hard-won victory of Jesus over sin and death, which enables us to enter with him into the divine blessedness where love reigns and all is restored. Francis Thompson writes in *The Hound of Heaven*: 'All which thy child's mistake / Fancies as lost, I have stored for thee at home. / Rise, clasp My hand, and come!' Hopkins urges us: 'Give beauty back, beauty, beauty, beauty, back to God, beauty's self and beauty's giver'. We are promised entry into the joy of God, and joy, as C. S. Lewis says, is the serious business of heaven!

Conversation with Jesus

You wait for Jesus to come today, aware now that each of his comings is a prelude to his final coming for me. You pray: 'Come, Lord Jesus!' (Revelation 22:20).

And he does come, smiling warmly. He says: 'Thank you for wanting me to come. Some day I will come and take you to myself forever. I promise you that, and I will not fail you.'

Perhaps you sit together in comfortable silence for a while. Perhaps you cry and he comforts you. You simply want to be with him whom you love, and he wants to be with you. You might say: 'You are my God, for you I long!' (Psalms 63:1, Grail version). He might reply: 'Love bids you welcome!'

To desire good relationships with God and one another is to be already in eternal life, and only the sleep of death will precede the splendour of its full unfolding. May we all meet there in God's good time! Amen.

Also by Brian Grogan SJ

Reflective Living
(with Una O'Connor. Messenger Publications 1986)

Love Beyond All Telling: An Introduction to the Mystery of God
(with Una O'Connor. Messenger Publications 1988)

Finding God in a New Age
(private printing 1993)

Finding God in All Things
(Messenger Publications 1996)

Our Graced Life-Stories
(Messenger Publications 2000)

Alone and on Foot – Ignatius of Loyola
(Veritas, Dublin, 2008)

Meetings Matter! – Spirituality and Skills for Meetings
(with Phyllis Brady. Veritas, Dublin, 2009)